KATRINA

Stories of Rescue, Recovery and Rebuilding in the Eye of the Storm

Edited by Susan M. Moyer

SP L.L.C.

www.SpotlightPress.com

ISBN: 1-59670-030-0

All photos by AP/Wide World Photos

Publishers	Peter L. Bannon and Joseph J. Bannon Sr.
Senior managing editor	Susan M. Moyer
Art director	K. Jeffrey Higgerson
Photo editor	Erin Linden-Levy
Book design and layout	Kenneth J. O'Brien and K. Jeffrey Higgerson
Cover design	Joseph T. Brumleve
Imaging	Heidi Norsen and Dustin Hubbart
Copy editor	Elisa Bock Laird
Media and promotions managers	Randy Fouts (national) and Maurey Williamson (print)

Printed in the United States of America

Spotlight Press L.L.C.
804 North Neil Street
Champaign, IL 61820

Phone 217.363.2072
Fax 217.363.2073

www.SpotlightPress.com

A portion of the proceeds from the sale of this book will go to the American Red Cross Disaster Relief Fund.

CONTENTS

PUBLISHER'S NOTE

What a difference we can make. If we take nothing else from the devastating events of Hurricane Katrina, let us continue to adopt the philosophy of compassion, generosity and selflessness that Americans are so willing to display at times when their fellow countrymen and -women are in dire need.

Hurricane Katrina left in its wake a trail of unimaginable destruction spanning the gulf coasts of Louisiana, Mississippi and Alabama. But it also left behind many incredible stories of courage and hope in the form of aid workers and volunteers rescuing those in need, and caring for those who lost everything. The compelling images of survival, rescue and relief stir our souls and empower us to do all that we can to help—through donations of money, goods, services, blood or time and energy.

We here at Spotlight Press are doing what we can as well. In response to the events of 9/11, we published in conjunction with the Associated Press a *New York Times* best-selling book, *America's Heroes: Inspiring Stories of Courage, Sacrifice and Patriotism.* Our book touched the hearts of people all across this great country. We received letters from readers thanking us for finding the "silver lining" in the unbelievable events of that day. In turn, we said thank you to the men and women who acted first on that day when we made a substantial contribution to the United Way's 9/11 Relief Fund.

Once again, we are honored to team up with many of the leading news sources around the country to publish *Katrina: Stories of Rescue, Recovery and Rebuilding in the Eye of the Storm.* In this book, we hope to again reveal the silver lining of this ruthless storm. We hope that this book will continue to encourage us to reach out to our fellow Americans in need.

As with *America's Heroes,* Spotlight Press will contribute a portion of the proceeds of this book to the Red Cross Disaster Relief Fund. Once more, it is our way of displaying how proud we are of our fellow Americans, who inspire us each and every day.

Sincerely,

Peter L. Bannon
Publisher

Gulf Coast braces for onslaught of Hurricane Katrina

By Associated Press

Across the South, preparations were being made as the region braced itself for the onslaught of Hurricane Katrina.

COVINGTON, Louisiana—The American Red Cross prepared a quarter-million meals to Baton Rouge, ready to bring them into New Orleans and surrounding parishes once Hurricane Katrina had passed. "We have a hundred response vehicles either in the Baton Rouge area or en route," said Kay Wilkins, the chief executive officer of the New Orleans chapter.

On Sunday, she headed from Covington, where the chapter's headquarters had temporarily relocated, to safer quarters 35 miles inland. Other staffers were heading to shelters in St. Tammany, Tangipahoa and Washington parishes. More than 2,000 refugees were staying in 16 Red Cross shelters all of them above Interstate 12, with 48 hours worth of supplies. Water trucks also were ready in Baton Rouge. But the aftermath will be a matter of weeks or months, not days. "We anticipate this is going to be a long-term disaster response," Wilkins said.

Above: In anticipation of Hurricane Katrina, Ron Julian boards up his store, Robinson's Antiques, on Royal Street in New Orleans.

Previous: Scott Kroehle and John Witherspoon batten down the hatches of a majestic New Orleans Garden District home.

NEW ORLEANS—Uptown New Orleans and other affluent areas were boarded up and deserted Sunday, with a few people packing their cars. In poorer parts of town, though, crowds of people were packing up and every store had long lines. Derbera Smith, 53, standing in one of those lines, said she wasn't leaving. "I'm staying right in my residence. What God has in store for us, that's what's going to happen. He can turn it around at the mouth of the Mississippi if He wants to," she said.

She said she blamed city officials for her danger because the housing project where she used to live was razed, and she now lives in an old wooden shotgun house. "We had a secure situation in that project," she said.

SURFSIDE BEACH, Texas—Thirteen surfers were pulled to safety off Quintana Beach on the Gulf of Mexico after becoming fatigued in 15-foot seas created by Katrina, the U.S. Coast Guard said. Troy Davis, a petty officer with the Coast Guard, said rip tides were strong Sunday. Most of the rescues occurred 400 to 500 yards offshore.

"That rip tide is real bad," surfer Gary Blanchard said. "It took me almost an hour to get in." Surfside Beach closed the Surfside jetties, used by many surfers as a launching point, Sunday evening. Surfside Beach is about 60 miles south of Houston. In addition, Gov. Rick Perry sent a 90-member urban search and rescue team to Louisiana to help out as the hurricane hits and in its aftermath.

ORANGE, Texas—Hundreds of Louisiana residents fleeing from Hurricane Katrina filled up shelters and hotels in southeast Texas. Janie Johnson, a service delivery manager with the American Red Cross chapter in Orange, described the steady flow of arrivals Sunday night as a "river of headlights." "They're tired and they've been on the road all day and they don't know what they're going home to," she said. More than 90 people had settled in at the First Baptist Church, where activities were set up for children. Once the shelter total reached 100, the First Presbyterian Church was set to open. Local veterinarian clinics and city animal control took care of the pets that residents had brought. Hotels also were filling up as evacuees headed west.

"We are 100 percent full," said Agatha Boniface, the assistant general manager of a Hampton Inn along Interstate 10, which connects New Orleans and Houston. She said they've been booked solid since Thursday, mostly with evacuees.

> ## "I'm staying right in my residence. What God has in store for us, that's what's going to happen."
> –Derbera Smith, New Orleans resident

MOBILE, Alabama—Jeff and Stephanie Taylor spent the night on the floor of Robertsdale High School with their 2-year-old son, Clay. "This one looks bad. We're not taking any chances," the man said as his son playfully threw a sandal in the air. Gov. Bob Riley earlier declared a state of emergency. Schools, bus lines and many businesses shut down in Mobile. Across the Mobile Bay, Baldwin County officials also braced for a storm surge and flooding at gulf resorts that are still recovering from Hurricane Ivan less than a year ago. The beachfront area of Gulf Shores and Orange Beach were under evacuation orders, and a line of heavy traffic, including boats being towed, headed north.

Gulf Shores Police Chief Arthur Bourne said the resort city would be under curfew all day Monday. The city was expected to be hit by winds of at least 80 mph through most of the day. As Katrina loomed, Katie Newton Collins and her husband, Jake, boarded up the family home on Alabama Pass in Orange Beach before heading toward their home in Birmingham. "When Ivan came through we said goodbye, and now this. It just keeps coming," she said.

GULFPORT, Mississippi—Before leaving, some locals walked along the shore to get a last glimpse of their beloved beaches. In 1969, powerful Hurricane Camille smashed the Mississippi coast, destroying homes and businesses well off the beach. "I just came down to see what it's like before because I know what it's going to look like after," said Joe Moffett, 34.

Nearby, a group of children frolicked in the choppy sea, enjoying some last moments in the warm Gulf before Katrina hits. Gov. Haley Barbour made a last-minute appeal for evacuations at a Sunday afternoon news conference in Jackson. He said all available resources were in place to deal with the storm's aftermath.

"This storm is going to have a statewide effect. This is not a coastal storm," Barbour said. He added that coastal residents should leave because "we are talking about a 30-foot wall of water. Take this seriously."

People along the coast were taking heed. Many of them compared Katrina to Camille. "I was here for Camille and I'm leaving," said Larry Anderson, 48, of Harrison County. "I was here and I remember it well. I don't want to be here for another one."

Above: This image, collected by NOAA at 4:15 a.m. EDT on August 25, 2005, shows Tropical Storm Katrina approaching the east coast of Florida.

Opposite: In hopes of saving his home from flooding, Arthur Allen fills sandbags in Morgan City, Louisiana.

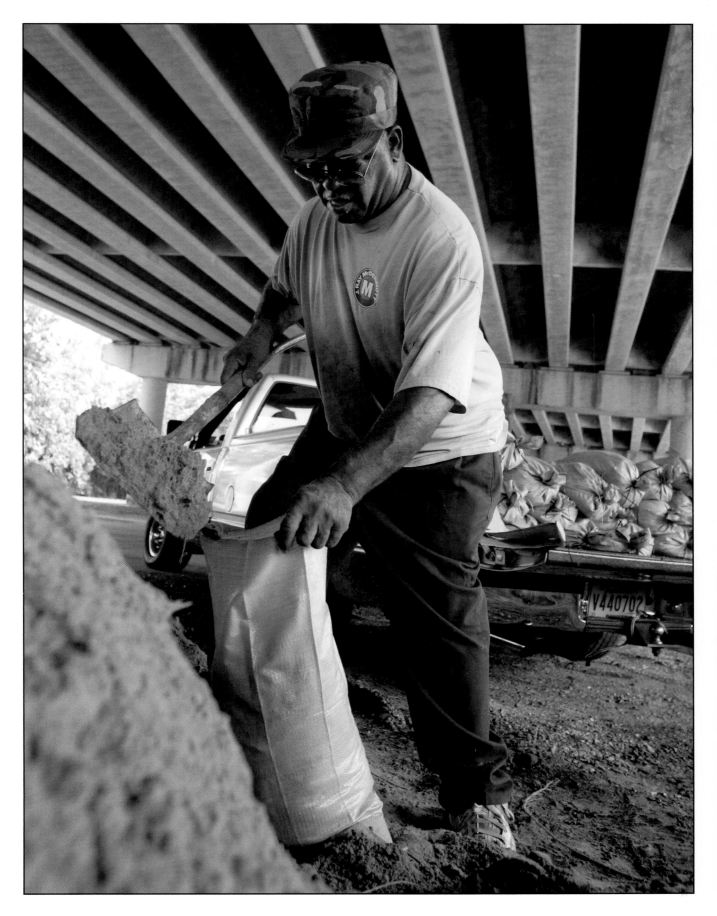

Katrina scares the party out of New Orleans

August 29, 2005
By Allen G. Breed, Associated Press

NEW ORLEANS—Tip Andrews knew it was time to leave when he saw the green shutters on the mustard-colored Cafe Lafitte, one of the French Quarter's most legendary bars.

"When they close, you KNOW it's bad," the Bourbon Street resident said yesterday as he took his two dogs, Gigi and Dijon, for a last walk before heading north. "They NEVER board up."

The Big Easy neighborhood famous for never sleeping was looking like a bar after last call Sunday as Hurricane Katrina barreled toward the Louisiana coast with 160-mph winds and a potential 28-foot storm surge.

The sickly sweet "hurricane" punch drinks that normally flow right up until landfall were nowhere to be seen as city workers did a last sweep of spent plastic cups and party debris. Purple, green and gold balloons fluttered forlornly on gas lamps in front of shuttered bars in the growing afternoon breeze.

"Where's everybody going?" a clearly besotted Edward Heyman shouted along an empty street. "It's just a little storm."

Despite his bravado, Heyman was leaving. But while some were taking the mandatory evacuation order seriously, many decided to stick it out and stare Katrina blearily in the face.

"You can sign my death certificate," cigar bar owner Michael Kincaid said, standing in line at Mattassa's corner grocery with a six-pack of beer, a bag of potato chips and a package of chocolate chip cookies. "My biggest investment is here, so I'm going to stay with it."

Roommates Michael Seward, 45, and Jesse Rowe, 28, went out yesterday to buy a battery-powered radio. They don't have a car to get out of town, but they feel perfectly safe in their second-story apartment.

"The house we live in was built for Napoleon's nephew," Seward said. "It's been here a while."

Seward pointed out that the Quarter was on some of the highest land in the city, "on the upper lip of the bowl."

Rowe said "hysterical" family and friends were calling to beg them to flee to Mississippi. Seward, who fled from Mississippi, quipped: "That's a fate worse than death."

Not everybody who stayed did so by choice.

Tim Smith, a machine technician from New York City, was in town for a family reunion when Katrina began its turn toward New Orleans. With no rental car and after several hours trying to get bus or train tickets, he decided to ride the storm out in his Bourbon Street hotel room.

"I was in 9-11," he said defiantly. "I mean, we're concerned, but we're not going to lose our minds over it. It's nature. Nature's got to take its course."

"Where's everybody going? It's just a little storm."

–Edward Heyman, New Orleans resident

Previous: Guietta Inscoe and Danny Norris board up a business in Pearl River, Louisiana.
Opposite: Vehicles jam the freeway as residents leave New Orleans and head inland to higher ground.

Left: Glenda Hall and Butch Bates pack up their fishing camp home on Lake Pontchartrain. The pair plan to head east to escape Hurricane Katrina.

Above: Sarah Vornholt and Aarica Stone play in the rough surf of Grande Lagoon in Pensacola, Florida, as the outer bands of Hurricane Katrina pass through the area.

"Nature's got to take its course."

—Tim Smith, New Orleans resident

New Orleans and Gulf Coast face grim forecast of expected devastation

August 27, 2005
By Susan Moyer

The National Weather Service issued a special statement in advance of Katrina's arrival outlining the damage that will likely be caused. If Hurricane Katrina makes landfall as a strong Category 4 or Category 5 storm, "most of the area will be uninhabitable for weeks, perhaps longer," said the statement. "At least one-half of well constructed homes will have roof and wall failure. All gabled roofs will fail, leaving those homes severely damaged or destroyed."

The National Weather Service warned that the majority of industrial buildings will become non-functional with partial or complete wall and roof failure. It went on to say that "All wood-framed, low-rise apartments will sustain major damage, including some wall and roof failure. Concrete block low-rise apartment will sustain major damage, including some wall and roof failure."

It is predicted that airborne debris will be widespread and may include heavy items, including household appliances, light cars and trucks. "The blown debris will create additional destruction, and persons, pets and livestock exposed to the winds will face certain death if struck." It is predicted that power outages will last for weeks because most power poles will be down and transformers will be destroyed. Most trees will be snapped or uprooted and even the heartiest, if they survive, will be stripped of all leaves.

Experts have warned about New Orleans' vulnerability for decades, mainly because Louisiana has lost more than a million acres of coastal wetlands in the past seven decades. The enormous patchwork of swamps and bayous south of the city serves as a buffer, partially absorbing the surge of water that a hurricane pushes ashore.

Many experts claim Katrina could turn New Orleans into a cesspool tainted with toxic chemicals, human waste and dangerous debris. It is feared that the levees and pumps that usually keep New Orleans dry have no chance against a direct hit by a Category 5 storm.

Other than Hurricane Andrew, which struck Miami in 1992, forecasters have no experience with Category 5 hurricanes hitting densely populated areas. Hurrying to put meteorological instruments in Katrina's path Sunday, wind engineers had little idea what their equipment would record.

Experts have also warned that the high levees surrounding New Orleans, which were designed to protect the city from floodwaters coming down the Mississippi, will only make things worse in a powerful hurricane. Katrina is expected to push a 28-foot storm surge against the levees. Even if they hold, water will pour over their tops and begin filling the city as if it were a sinking canoe.

> ### "Most of the area will be uninhabitable for weeks, perhaps longer."
> —National Weather Service

It has been 40 years since New Orleans faced a hurricane even comparable to Katrina. In 1965, Hurricane Betsy, a Category 3 storm, submerged some parts of the city to a depth of 7 feet.

Since then, the Big Easy has been lucky, suffering only near misses. In 1998, Hurricane Georges was headed directly for New Orleans, but swerved at the last minute and struck Mississippi and Alabama. Hurricane Lili dissipated at the mouth of the Mississippi in 2002. And in 2004, Hurricane Ivan curved to the east as it came ashore, saving New Orleans from devastation.

Previous: Loranie Keane leaves Katrina a message as she prepares her Loxley, Alabama, business for the storm.
Opposite: Waves crash against the sea wall in Orange Beach, Alabama, as Hurricane Katrina strengthens into a Category 5 storm.

"The bottom line is this is a worst-case scenario and everybody needs to recognize it. You can always rebuild your house, but you can never regain a life. And there's no point risking your life and the lives of your children."

–Ivor van Heerden, LSU Hurricane Center

Below: Traffic along Highway 90 leaving Morgan City, Louisiana, is at a standstill as residents attempt to evacuate the Gulf Coast.

Right: Hurricane specialist Stacy Stewart looks grim as he studies data related to Hurricane Katrina before the storm made landfall.

17

Thousands flock to the safety of Superdome

August 28, 2005
By Mary Foster, Associated Press

NEW ORLEANS—For nearly 35,000 of this city's poor, homeless and frail just getting into the massive Louisiana Superdome and hunkering down was the hardest part. The sickest among them didn't flee the wrath of Hurricane Katrina on Sunday as much as they hobbled to safety on crutches and canes, and came in on stretchers. Others lined up for blocks, clutching meager belongings and crying children as National Guardsmen searched them for guns, knives and drugs.

"We just took the necessities," said Michael Skipper, who pulled a wagon loaded with bags of clothes and a radio. "The good stuff—the television and the furniture—you just have to hope something's there when you get back. If it's not, you just start over."

Then the rain began, heavy and steady. It drenched the many people still outside, along with their blankets and the bags of food and clothing they clutched.

"I know it's going to be a miserable night. It's already been a miserable night. But what can we do?" 44-year-old Kris Benson said.

New Orleans' most frail residents got priority for placement in the makeshift Superdome shelter, by far the most solid of the Big Easy's 10 refuges of last resort for the estimated 100,000 city residents who don't have the means or strength to join a mandatory evacuation.

By nightfall, an estimated 25,000 to 35,000 heeded the call.

Above: Nine-year-old Destiny Mitchell; her mother, Sabrina Houston (right); her great-grandmother, Elsie Houston (seated at center) and her grandmother, Jonetta Houston (standing at center), wait to enter the Louisiana Superdome.
Previous: People seek shelter in the Superdome in anticipation of the hurricane.

The dome, with its bare floor and stadium seats, is likely to end up their home for the next few days as the hurricane hits and the region deals with its aftermath.

"They told us not to stay in our houses because it wasn't safe," said 76-year-old Victoria Young, who sat amid plastic bags and a metal walker. "It's not safe anywhere when you're in the shape we're in."

Curtis Cockran, 54, a diabetic who recently had hip surgery, sat in his wheelchair on a loading dock at the dome while nurses, emergency technicians and doctors attended to evacuees' needs.

"I just want a place I can be quiet and left alone," he said. "I don't know if I'll have a place to go back to, but there's no reason to worry about that now. For the time being I just want to be safe."

More serious cases had to be taken to other cities in Louisiana for medical care.

"There are some conditions we just can't handle here," said Dr. Kevin Stephens, the head of New Orleans' health department. "Like dialysis. We can't do that, and they'll be here three or four days, so they'll need it before then."

The 77,000-seat stadium, home to the NFL's New Orleans Saints and New Year's Sugar Bowl game, provided few comforts but at least had bathrooms for the evacuees and food donated by several charities.

Above: Thousands of displaced residents take cover from Hurricane Katrina at the Superdome.

"They may be here for a while," said Gen. Ralph Lupin, the National Guardsman in charge of the shelter. "The electricity will be out after the storm; streets will be almost impassable. So once they get here, they'll have to stay for the duration."

Guardsmen made able-bodied people clasp their hands behind their backs while they patted them down, feeling the seams and hems of clothing, and then ran metal detectors over them. The backpacks, suitcases and plastic grocery bags that held their belongings were searched.

Alice George, 76, a homeless woman wearing shorts and a T-shirt with the word *Love* on the front, was searched for almost 10 minutes.

"They took my cigarettes and lighter," she said. "I guess I'll do without."

Joey Branson wasn't worried. The 42-year-old breezed through the search with just a fresh apple pie and a paperback mystery.

"That's all I need," he said, smiling. "I'm set for the duration."

Above: In the Superdome, National Guardsmen distribute ready-to-eat meals to the evacuees.
Opposite: The seats of the Superdome are filled with New Orleans residents.

Katrina floods the Big Easy, moves inland with a vengeance

August 29, 2005
By Allen G. Breed, Associated Press

Announcing itself with shrieking 145-mph winds, Hurricane Katrina slammed into the Gulf Coast just outside New Orleans on Monday, submerging entire neighborhoods up to their roofs, swamping Mississippi's beachfront casinos and blowing out windows in hospitals, hotels and high-rises.

For New Orleans—a dangerously vulnerable city because it sits mostly below sea level in a bowl-shaped depression—it was not the apocalyptic storm forecasters had feared.

But it was plenty bad, in New Orleans and elsewhere along the coast, where scores people had to be rescued from rooftops and attics as the floodwaters rose around them.

At least five deaths were blamed on Katrina—three people killed by falling trees in Mississippi and two killed in a traffic accident in Alabama. And an untold number of other people were feared dead in flooded neighborhoods, many of which could not be reached by rescuers because of high water.

"Some of them, it was their last night on Earth," Terry Ebbert, the chief of homeland security for New Orleans, said of people who ignored orders to evacuate the city of 480,000 over the weekend. "That's a hard way to learn a lesson."

"We pray that the loss of life is very limited, but we fear that is not the case," Louisiana Gov. Kathleen Blanco said.

Katrina knocked out power to more than three-quarters of a million people from Louisiana to the Florida's Panhandle, and authorities said it could be two months before electricity is restored to everyone. Ten major hospitals in New Orleans were running on emergency backup power.

As of Monday evening, Katrina was passing through southeast Mississippi, moving north at 18 mph. It had weakened into a mere Category 1 hurricane with winds near 75 mph.

But it was far from done: Forecasters said that as the storm moves north through the nation's midsection over the next few days, it may spawn tornadoes over the Southeast and swamp the Gulf Coast and the Tennessee and Ohio valleys with a potentially ruinous 8 inches or more of rain.

Katrina had menaced the Gulf Coast over the weekend as a 175-mph, Category 5 monster, the most powerful ranking on the scale. But it weakened to a Category 4 and made a slight right-hand turn just become it came ashore around daybreak near the Louisiana bayou town of Buras, passing just east of New Orleans on a path that spared the Big Easy—and its fabled French Quarter—from its full fury.

In nearby coastal St. Bernard Parish, Katrina's storm surge swamped an estimated 40,000 homes. In a particularly low-lying neighborhood on the south shore of Lake Ponchartain, a levee along a canal gave way and forced dozens of residents to flee or scramble to the roofs when water rose to their gutters.

"I've never encountered anything like it in my life. It just kept rising and rising and rising," said Bryan Vernon, who spent three hours on his roof, screaming over howling winds for someone to save him and his fiancée.

Across a street that had turned into a river bobbing with garbage cans, trash and old tires, a woman leaned from the second-story window of a brick home and pleaded to be rescued.

"We pray that the loss of life is very limited, but we fear that is not the case."

–Louisiana Gov. Kathleen Blanco

Previous: In downtown New Orleans, an American flag is battered in the high winds and rain of Hurricane Katrina.
Opposite: Cars sit abandoned on New Orleans streets as the floodwaters rise.

Above: A boat is washed onto Highway 90 as Hurricane Katrina hits Gulfport, Mississippi.

"There are three kids in here," the woman said. "Can you help us?"

Blanco said 200 people have been rescued in boats from rooftops, attics and other locations around the New Orleans area, a scene playing out in Mississippi as well. In some cases, rescuers are sawing through roofs to get to people in attics, and other stranded residents "are swimming to our boats," the governor said.

Elsewhere along the Gulf Coast, Mississippi was subjected to both Katrina's harshest winds and highest recorded storm surges—22 feet. The storm pushed water up to the second floor of homes, flooded floating casinos, uprooted hundreds of trees and flung sailboats across a highway.

"Let me tell you something, folks: I've been out there. It's complete devastation," said Gulfport, Miss., Fire Chief Pat Sullivan.

In Gulfport, young children clung to one another in a small blue boat as neighbors shuffled children and elderly residents out of a flooded neighborhood.

"Everything is flooded. Roofs are off and everything," said Shun Howell, 25, who was trying to leave with her 5-year-old son. "Everything is ruined."

In some cases, debris was stacked 4 to 5 feet, covering cars. Houses were washed from their foundations.

In Alabama, Katrina's arrival was marked by the flash and crackle of exploding transformers. The hurricane toppled huge oak branches on Mobile's waterfront and broke apart an oil-drilling platform, sending a piece slamming into a major bridge.

Muddy 6-foot waves crashed into the eastern shore of Mobile Bay, flooding stately antebellum mansions and littering them with oak branches.

"There are lots of homes through here worth a million dollars. At least they were yesterday," said a shirtless Fred Wright. "I've been here 25 years, and this is the worst I've ever seen the water."

Katrina also shattered scores of windows in high-rise office buildings and on five floors of the Charity Hospital, forcing patients to be moved to lower levels. White curtains that had been sucked out of the shattered windows of a hotel became tangled in treetops.

In the French Quarter, made up of Napoleonic-era buildings with wrought-iron balconies, the damage was relatively light.

On Jackson Square, two massive oak trees outside the 278-year-old St. Louis Cathedral came out by the roots, ripping out a 30-foot section of ornamental iron fence and straddling a marble statue of Jesus Christ, snapping off the thumb and forefinger of his outstretched hand.

At the hotel Le Richelieu, the winds blew open sets of balcony French doors shortly after dawn. Seventy-three-year-old Josephine Elow pressed her weight against the broken doors as a hotel employee tried to secure them.

"It's not life-threatening," she said as rainwater dripped from her face. "God's got our back."

"I've been here 25 years, and this is the worst I've ever seen the water."

−Fred Wright, Mobile Bay, Alabama resident

Above: Floodwaters rise as Hurricane Katrina moves through the Gulf Coast.

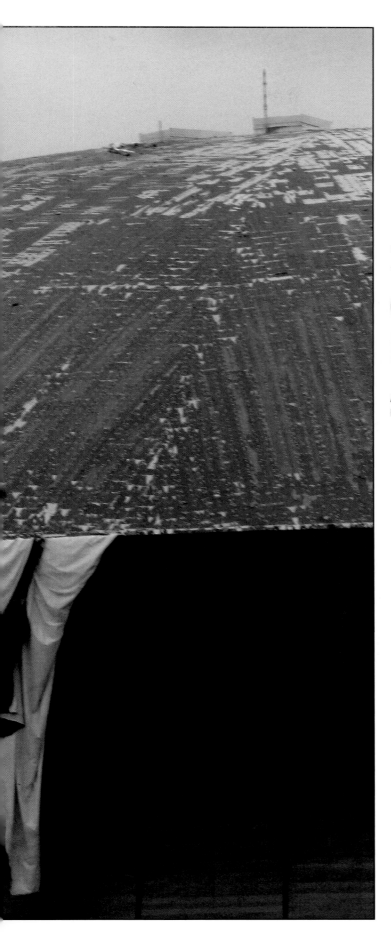

Superdome roof damaged by Katrina

August 29, 2005
By Susan Moyer

NEW ORLEANS—The evacuees who took shelter in the New Orleans Superdome couldn't completely escape the wrath of Hurricane Katrina. The Louisiana Superdome, where approximately 10,000 people have taken refuge from Hurricane Katrina, reportedly began leaking as winds damaged the roof, letting daylight and rainwater in the darkened arena.

Frightened evacuees with few belongings and crying children braved the conditions after the power went out, turning the building into a hot and muggy discomfort zone. Then part of the roof blew off. Strips of metal peeled away, creating two large holes visible from the floor of the immense arena. Evacuees watched as sheets of metal were visibly flapping wildly and noisily. The holes were in an area of vents some 19 stories above the arena floor.

"We think the wind somehow got into the vents and got between the roof's [waterproof] membrane and the aluminum ceiling tiles," said Doug Thornton, the regional manager of the company that manages the huge arena.

Said Ed Reams of WDSU-TV in New Orleans: "I can see daylight straight up from inside the Superdome. This is only going to get bigger. We have another two hours before the worst of the storm gets to us."

Superdome officials and Louisiana Gov. Kathleen Blanco assured residents that the Superdome is not in danger, stressing that they did not expect the huge roof to fail because of the relatively small breaches, each about 15 to 20 feet long and 4 to 5 feet wide.

"This is only going to get bigger. We have another two hours before the worst of the storm gets to us."

—Ed Reams, WDSU-TV, New Orleans

Inside the home of the New Orleans Saints, the National Guard moved people to the other side of the dome, while others were relocated beneath concrete-reinforced seats on the terrace level.

In addition to the two holes, water was leaking in through many other areas, including elevators and stairwells, as the wind forced water in through any small opening. Across Poydras Street, numerous shattered windows were visible on high-rise office buildings.

The problem started with a leak and grew larger until sounds of the roof banging could be heard. Authorities could not fix the problem in the middle of the storm, but the command center was on stand-by with resources. Superdome officials attempted to keep evacuees dry until Hurricane Katrina passed through and they were able to assess the damage to the dome's roof.

Power finally failed at about 5 a.m. Monday morning. Emergency generators quickly kicked in. Unfortunately, they only run reduced lighting, not the air-conditioning system. The inside of the Superdome quickly became very hot, and condensation made some floors wet and slippery. Refugees were not allowed to accommodate themselves on the football field in case flooding occurred.

Katrina's full wrath still being felt as body count rises

August 30, 2005
By Hobrook Mohr, Associated Press

GULFPORT, Mississippi—Rescuers in boats and helicopters searched for survivors of Hurricane Katrina and brought victims to shelters Tuesday as the extent of the damage across the Gulf of Mexico coast became ever clearer. The governor said the death toll in one Mississippi county alone could be as high as 80.

"The devastation down there is just enormous," Gov. Haley Barbour said on NBC's *Today* show, the morning after Katrina howled ashore with winds of 145 mph and engulfed thousands of homes in one of the most punishing storms on record in the United States.

In New Orleans, meanwhile, water began rising in the streets Tuesday morning, apparently because of a break on a levee along a canal leading to Lake Pontchartrain. New Orleans lies mostly below sea level and is protected by a network of pumps, canals and levees. Many of the pumps were not working Tuesday morning.

Officials planned to use helicopters to drop 3,000-pound sandbags into the breach.

Barbour said there were unconfirmed reports of up to 80 deaths in Harrison County—which includes devastated Gulfport and Biloxi—and the number was likely to rise. At least five other deaths across the Gulf Coast were blamed on Katrina.

Above: New Orleans residents wait to be rescued from their flooded homes.
Previous: Truckloads of people arrive at the Superdome after being evacuated from rooftops and flooded areas.

"We know that there is a lot of the coast that we have not been able to get to," the governor said. "I hate to say it, but it looks like it is a very bad disaster in terms of human life."

Along the Gulf Coast, tree trunks, downed power lines and trees, and chunks of broken concrete in the streets prevented rescuers from reaching victims. Swirling water in many areas contained hidden dangers. Crews worked to clear highways. Along one Mississippi highway, motorists themselves used chainsaws to remove trees blocking the road.

"What we're doing is trying to make the best of a bad situation, and we need people to cooperate," New Orleans Police Chief Eddie Compass said.

More than 1,600 Mississippi National Guardsmen were activated to help with the recovery, and the Alabama Guard planned to send two battalions to Mississippi.

In New Orleans, a city of 480,000 that was mostly evacuated over the weekend as Katrina closed in, those who stayed behind faced another, delayed threat: rising water. Failed pumps and levees apparently sent water from Lake Pontchartrain coursing through the streets.

The rising water forced one New Orleans hospital to move patients to the Louisiana Superdome, where some 10,000 people had taken shelter, authorities said.

In downtown New Orleans, streets that were relatively clear in the hours after the storm were filled with 1 foot to 1½ feet of water Tuesday morning. Water was knee-deep around the Superdome. Canal Street was literally a canal. Water lapped at the edge of the French Quarter.

"We know that last night we had over 300 folks that we could confirm were on tops of roofs and waiting for our assistance. We pushed hard all throughout the night. We hoisted over 100 folks last night just in the Mississippi area. Our crews over New Orleans probably did twice that," Capt. Dave Callahan of the Coast Guard Aviation Training Center in Mississippi said on ABC.

National Guardsmen brought in people from outlying areas to the Superdome in the backs of big 2½-ton Army trucks. Louisiana's wildlife enforcement department also brought people in on the backs of their pickups. Some were wet, some were in wheelchairs, some were holding babies and nothing else.

> *"We pushed hard all throughout the night. We hoisted over 100 folks last night just in the Mississippi area."*
> —Capt. Dave Callahan, Coast Guard Aviation Training Center in Mississippi

Louisiana Gov. Kathleen Blanco said on ABC: "The biggest concern is that this whole situation is totally overwhelming. I know the desperation of all of the folks who had evacuated. I know they desperately want to get in. In most cases, it is totally impossible for them to get in. The streets are inundated with water. The devastation is vast. And there's really—there's nothing they can do."

In Louisiana, Terry Ebbert, New Orleans' homeland security chief, said bodies were seen floating in the floodwaters in the hardest-hit areas. He could not give an estimate of deaths as of Tuesday morning, but said he believed the death toll would not be as great as some of the images of devastation would suggest.

The death toll does not include 11 deaths in South Florida when a much-weaker Katrina first hit land last week.

"My parents always told me when waters are going to rise, never stay in New Orleans because it is already below sea level and the levees will not hold up."

–New Orleans college student and evacuee

Teresa Kavanagh, 35, of Biloxi, shook her head is disbelief as she took photographs of the damage in her hometown.

"Total devastation. Apartment complexes are wiped clean. We're going to rebuild, but it's going to take long time. Houses that withstood Camille are nothing but slab now," she said. Hurricane Camille killed 256 people in Louisiana and Mississippi in 1969.

In Biloxi the mayor's office said the storm's surge put at least five casinos out of commission. The Hard Rock Cafe and Beau Rivage were severely damaged. The bottom floors of a condominium were all but washed away. All that remained of one hotel was the toilets.

Katrina's surge also demolished major bridges along the coast. The storm swept sailboats onto city streets in Gulfport and obliterated hundreds of waterfront homes, businesses, community landmarks and condominiums.

The hurricane knocked out power to more than 1 million people from Louisiana to Florida, and authorities said it could be two months before electricity is restored to everyone. Katrina also disrupted petroleum output in the very center of the U.S. oil refining industry and rattled energy markets.

According to preliminary assessments by AIR Worldwide Corp., a risk assessment company, the insurance industry faces as much as $26 billion in claims from Katrina.

Above: Parish councilman Joe Impastato (front left), firemen Robert Artigue, Dana Hall, Gary Artigue, Dan Flynn, Mark Frosch and a good Samaritan help evacuate a resident from his flooded home in Lacombe, Louisiana.

Opposite: Slot machines are visible in a Biloxi, Mississippi, casino demolished by Hurricane Katrina.

That would make Katrina more expensive than the previous record-setting storm, Hurricane Andrew, which caused some $21 billion in insured losses in 1992 to property in Florida and along the Gulf Coast.

Michael Brown, the director of the Federal Emergency Management Agency, said on CBS that it will be "quite awhile" before those displaced by the hurricane can return, particularly in areas close to downtown New Orleans. In some places, "it's going to be weeks at least before people can get back."

And once the floodwaters go down, "it's going to be incredibly dangerous" because of structural damage to homes, diseases from animal carcasses and chemicals in homes, Brown said.

Authorities said there was also a levee breach in the western part of the city. Jason Binet, of the Army Corps of Engineers, said that breach began Monday afternoon and may have grown overnight.

"I thought I was doing good. Then I noticed my Jeep was under water."

–Scott Radish, New Orleans resident

"The hurricane was scary," Scott Radish told New Orleans newspaper *The Times-Picayune*. "All the tree branches fell, but the building stood. I thought I was doing good. Then I noticed my Jeep was under water."

Across the Gulf Coast, people were rescued as they clung to rooftops, hundreds of trees were uprooted and sailboats were flung about like toys when Katrina crashed ashore Monday in what could become the most expensive storm in U.S. history.

Mississippi's economy was also dealt a blow that could run into the millions, as the storm shuttered the flashy casinos that dot its coast. The gambling houses are built on barges anchored just off the beach, and Barbour said emergency officials had received reports of water reaching the third floors of some casinos.

At New Orleans' Superdome, where power was lost early Monday, some 10,000 refugees spent a second night in the dark bleachers. With the air conditioning off, the carpets were soggy, the bricks were slick with humidity and anxiety was rising.

"Everybody wants to go see their house. We want to know what's happened to us. It's hot, it's miserable and, on top of that, you're worried about your house," said Rosetta Junne, 37.

Above: Tearing free of their moorings at a Pascagoula, Mississippi, marina, boats have been run aground during the hurricane.

Opposite, top: A car is partially submerged in the swimming pool of a home destroyed by Hurricane Katrina in Biloxi, Mississippi.

Opposite, bottom: A demolished car stands on the side of a New Orleans street.

Above: Water surges over a broken levee near downtown.

Opposite: A firefighter wades through knee-deep water to help battle a building fire in downtown New Orleans. The flooding made it difficult for firefighters to respond.

Katrina survivors face horror, hope

September 1, 2005
By Allen G. Breed, Associated Press

NEW ORLEANS—Set down on dry land after three days cowering atop furniture in her flooded kitchen, 83-year-old Camille Fletcher stumbled a few feet and collapsed. She and two of her children had made it through Hurricane Katrina alive, but her Glendalyn with the long, beautiful black hair was gone.

"My precious daughter," Fletcher sobbed Wednesday. "I prayed to God to keep us safe in His loving care."

Then, looking into an incongruously blue sky, she whimpered: "You're supposed to be a loving God. You're supposed to love us. And what have You done to us? Why did You do this to us?"

But for the rescuers who plucked Fletcher and untold others from roofs, balconies and highways flooded by Hurricane Katrina, such questions were a luxury they simply could not afford.

Emergency officials say 72 hours is about the longest they can expect most people to last in the sweltering Louisiana heat. So they called in volunteers from across this "fisherman's paradise" to help improve the survivors' odds.

Ronnie Lovett and about 30 of his crew from R&R Construction drove four hours from Sulphur, La., to join the rescue effort. They arose with the sun Wednesday after spending the night in sleeping bags on the pavement outside Harrah's casino on the Mississippi River, because they couldn't find rooms.

Lovett is paying the men's wages and furnishing gas for their personal boats.

"They're all Bubbas, swamp men," said Lovett, who brought his own 21-foot fishing boat. "We're here for the duration, until they turn us loose."

At dawn, a motley armada of air boats, aluminum skiffs and even a two-seater Jet Ski moved out from the central business district. Heading east in the westbound lanes of Interstate 10, the boats passed the Superdome, where hundreds of ragged people stood on the hot pavement and helicopters buzzed around.

"I need to get me to some high ground, I wasn't born with fins."

—Simon Queen, New Orleans resident

Many of the displaced had clearly spent the night on the highway rather than suffer the stable-like conditions of the sports stadium. The caravan passed people dragging suitcases and pushing shopping carts. One man waved an empty water jug like a railroad lantern, pleading for someone to stop and fill it.

After nearly an hour of zigzagging around downed lampposts and plowing through water up to past their wheel wells, the volunteer navy arrived at a staging point in New Orleans East, just south of Lake Pontchartrain.

New Orleans Police Officer Martin Jules warned the men not to overload their boats. Some volunteers have had their rigs taken from them at gunpoint, so Jules also warned them not to be heroes.

"These people have been out here two or three days," he said, standing on the bow of a flatboat. "They're scared, they're tired, they're thirsty, they're hungry. If it gets hostile, we roll, OK? We're here to help 'em. We got to be here to help them for the next couple of months, however long it takes. Our safety is No. 1."

Within minutes of launching, the men were returning with sunken-eyed, sallow-skinned survivors.

The boats circled a Day's Inn, where people had hung sheets on the balconies reading, "SOS" and "We need food and water." At Forest Tower, a high-rise senior citizens apartment complex, one man waved his empty oxygen tank out a window.

A boat floated through the building's shattered entrance and pulled right up to the stairs. Elderly residents stepped gingerly onto tables and into the boats.

Simon Queen, 68, said he slept through Hurricane Betsy. But Katrina was like "King Kong pounding at the windows."

"I need to get me to some high ground," he said. "I wasn't born with fins."

At the nearby United Medical Rehab Hospital, 14 patients, 11 staff members and their families awaited their saviors.

Nurse Bernadette Shine said the facility was nearly out of oxygen, and several diabetic patients had been without dialysis for nearly a week. After the fruit cocktail and peanut butter ran out, the staff broke into the candy and drink machines for sugary items to keep patients from going into shock.

"There are people that are not going to make it," Shine said, her voice cracking. "One I've known since I was 10 years old. But we did what we could for them. We did everything we could for them."

After several hours, a small fleet of rented moving trucks showed up to take the people to the downtown convention center so they could be taken out of the city. Police herded people up metal ramps like cattle into the unrefrigerated boxes.

Above: Bryan Vernon and Dorothy Bell are rescued from their rooftop after rising water stranded them there.
Previous: An old rowboat is used to evacuate children and an elderly woman from their flooded homes in Gulfport, Mississippi.

Camille Fletcher sat forlorn, not really caring when it would be her turn. Suddenly, a woman emerged from the waters and began walking toward her. She had long, disheveled black hair.

"Mamma?" she shouted.

"Oh my God, oh my God," the old woman screamed, kissing Glendalyn's hand and pressing it against her forehead. "My daughter's alive!"

The 59-year-old Glendalyn Fletcher told her family a harrowing story of how she had floated through a wall at her house a mile away from her mother's and swum, stripped naked by the raging torrent, to a neighbor's house and cowered in an attic; how someone had picked them up Tuesday and left them stranded on a waterlocked section of I-10.

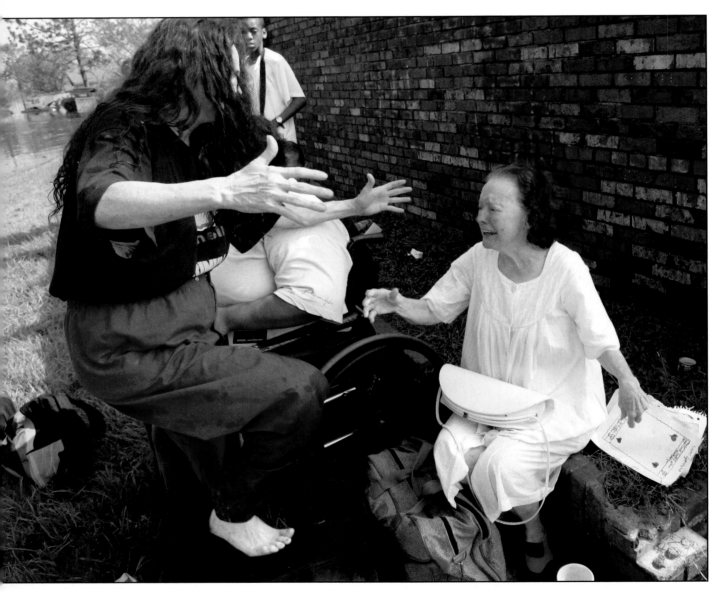

Above: Camille Fletcher (right) and her daughter Glendalyn are tearfully reunited after being separated by surging floodwaters.

"It was horrible, but there were millions of stars," the dehydrated woman said.

A few moments later, it was time for Camille Fletcher to go to a shelter. Before being helped into the back of the moving truck, she looked back at her daughter and smiled.

"God is good."

Above: Garron Lenaz recovers an American flag from the rubble in front of his home in Gulfport, Mississippi.

Above: Sammuel Dunn (center) is helped to safety by friends after he was rescued by boat from his flooded home.

Left: Evacuating their Lacombe, Louisiana, home, Adeline Perkins and Lynell Batiste carry their dogs, Princess and Timmy, through chest-high floodwaters while Kewanda Batiste and Ulysses Batiste swim behind them.

Opposite: Leaving their homes and businesses behind, residents walk up submerged Canal Street in New Orleans.

"I told my wife that from now on when she mentions the stuff that was left behind in the storm, she must end each statement with 'Oh, well.'"

–Katrina survivor

Buzz of helicopters replaces jazz in once vibrant New Orleans

September 6, 2005
By AFP

NEW ORLEANS (AFP)—The once jazzy and vibrant streets of New Orleans have new sounds: the buzz of helicopters and rumble of rescue convoys.

Hurricane Katrina has quieted the jazz capital with its cataclysmic floods, possibly leaving thousands dead in the city that once housed nearly 500,000 people.

The killer storm has brought wind, water and fire to the city where a raucous Mardi Gras festival is celebrated every year. Columns of black smoke rise above the skyline. A helicopter tries to douse a burning house as firefighters below pump black water into the blaze. Elsewhere, a church is engulfed by flames.

On bridges and elevated roads, ambulances and columns of rescuers look for survivors and urge those who chose to stay to leave, as most of the city remains partially submerged.

"Some want to go, some want to stay, a big percentage said no, they don't want to go," said Capt. Richard Gully, of the Texas Parks and Wildlife department.

"A disaster of this scale is overwhelming," Gully said, staring into the distance. His team includes 4x4 vehicles and airboats.

The water is being drained out of the streets. In one part of the city, a team pumps the sullied water to clear the road to the Louis Armstrong International Airport, which was turned into a rescue base. Elsewhere, soldiers clear trees from streets.

The task ahead is of titanic proportions. Some progress has come to light: New Orleans Mayor Ray Nagin said 60 percent of his city was underwater, down from 80 percent last week.

Power has returned in some parts of the city's outskirts. Some businesses have reopened, selling generators and fuel. The Ochsner hospital offers consultations since Tuesday.

AP Photo/Ron Haviv/VII

The eery atmosphere is mixed with surreal scenes.

U.S. soldiers from the 82nd Airborne Division, which served in Iraq and were brought in to help police the city, displayed combat zone instincts as they took cover behind doors or trees whenever a car moved.

Authorities says alligators are stalking the flooded waters and rescuers fear that they will eat the bodies of the hurricane victims.

Residents have a hard time envisioning what lays ahead. Most have fled the city, but a few have stayed behind.

Dwight Whitfield chose to stay with his dog G in his little house in a plush neighborhood spared by the floods.

"I'd like to give a hand, putting the city back together," said Whitfield, 37, who worked for a power company. "Now I just sit around, I walk my dog. I want to do something but I prefer to be directed. I don't want to be in anybody's way."

"One day at a time, you can't plan for anything, you just deal with it," he said.

Bobby Comeaux, who took his family to Dallas, Texas, returned to his neighborhood in Jefferson Parish when authorities allowed residents to take stock of the damage. His home was mucked by 12-inch high water.

Comeaux, who has already enrolled his children in a Texas school, packed pictures and frames into his car. Will he return to once musical New Orleans?

"I don't know," he said. "I don't think anybody does."

> *"One day at a time, you can't plan for anything, you just deal with it."*
>
> —Dwight Whitfield, New Orleans resident

Above: Search and rescue personnel go house to house looking for survivors of Hurricane Katrina.
Previous: Ted Mack sits outside a bar on Bourbon Street in the all-but-deserted French Quarter in New Orleans.

AP Photo/Ron Haviv/VII

"So many have lost so much. Best we can do is go back as soon as they'll let us and use our good luck and what we have to help those who weren't as fortunate."

—Katrina survivor

Rescuers turn their attention to New Orleans' pets

September 12, 2005
By AFP

BATON ROUGE, Louisiana (ANTARA News/AFP)—Soldiers assigned to rescue survivors of Hurricane Katrina in New Orleans are turning their attention to saving pets as the number of people being plucked to safety dwindles.

"Our focus so far is on people but ... there is a lot of focus and concerns of a lot of people who left their animals or became separated from them," said Lt. Gen. Russel Honore, the commander of the Katrina rescue operation here.

"We've got the capacity, it seemed like the right thing to do," he told reporters in the Louisiana capital of Baton Rouge.

Animal rescue officials have been collecting scores of pets and other animals from the shattered city, while many survivors have told of their distress at having to leave beloved cats and dogs behind in the watery city when they fled.

The tens of thousands of troops that have secured the city are completing their operation to rescue stranded victims and are now focusing on evacuating remaining residents and receiving bodies, Honore said.

TIPS FOR TAKING CARE OF PETS DURING EMERGENCY EVACUATIONS

Many dogs, cats and other animals were left behind by hurricane evacuees and victims. They need food, water, shelter and possibly medical treatment. Experts say animals, like people, experience significant trauma during disasters. In addition, horses and other hooved animals that stand in water for great lengths of time can develop hoof and leg problems. Here are some ways to protect your animals in times of emergency.

WORK OUT A BUDDY SYSTEM

The ASPCA recommends creating a buddy system. Exchange house keys with a trusted neighbor, friend, relative or pet sitter so you can care for each other's animals in a disaster situation. Ask relatives and friends outside your area if they'd be willing to take you and your pets in if you ever need to evacuate. Try to line up several options if you have multiple pets that could overwhelm a single household.

IF YOU ARE HOME AND ARE ORDERED TO EVACUATE, TAKE YOUR PETS WITH YOU IF AT ALL POSSIBLE

The ASPCA advises people to get in their cars with their animals and start driving. Eventually they will come across someone who will offer assistance. But if you leave pets behind and you get down the road and think, "You know, that probably wasn't the best thing to do; I'm going to go back and get the dog," they're not going to let you back in.

INVESTIGATE IN ADVANCE SHELTER OPTIONS

Most shelters don't permit pets, but the Humane Society of the United States reports pet-friendly shelters are sometimes available. Even if a shelter doesn't allow pets, your animals can stay in your car and you can go out to care for them as needed. You may also choose to take refuge at a hotel where pets are permitted.

Above: An abandoned dog is rescued in New Orleans.
Previous: Carrying his dog, Cuddles, Jonathan Harvey wades from his flooded home.

BECOME FAMILIAR WITH AREA RESOURCES

Know all of the veterinary hospitals, boarding kennels, animal rescue organizations and pet-friendly hotels outside your area. You might need to shelter your pets with them someday, so keep their 24-hour emergency numbers on hand for quick reference.

DON'T FENCE THEM IN

If your pets are left behind inadvertently or because there's no alternative, give them a fighting chance by making sure they're not chained or penned up and that they are wearing identification so they can be reunited with you if found. Pets at home alone in the event of a disaster will do their best to survive.

Above: New Orleans evacuee Ruby Herpin is reunited with Sweetie, one of her five rescued cats, at the South Chattanooga Recreation Center in Tennessee.

Above: U.S. Army Chief Warrant Officer Dan Langdon from Fort Hood, Texas, comforts a stray dog after landing his Chinook helicopter.

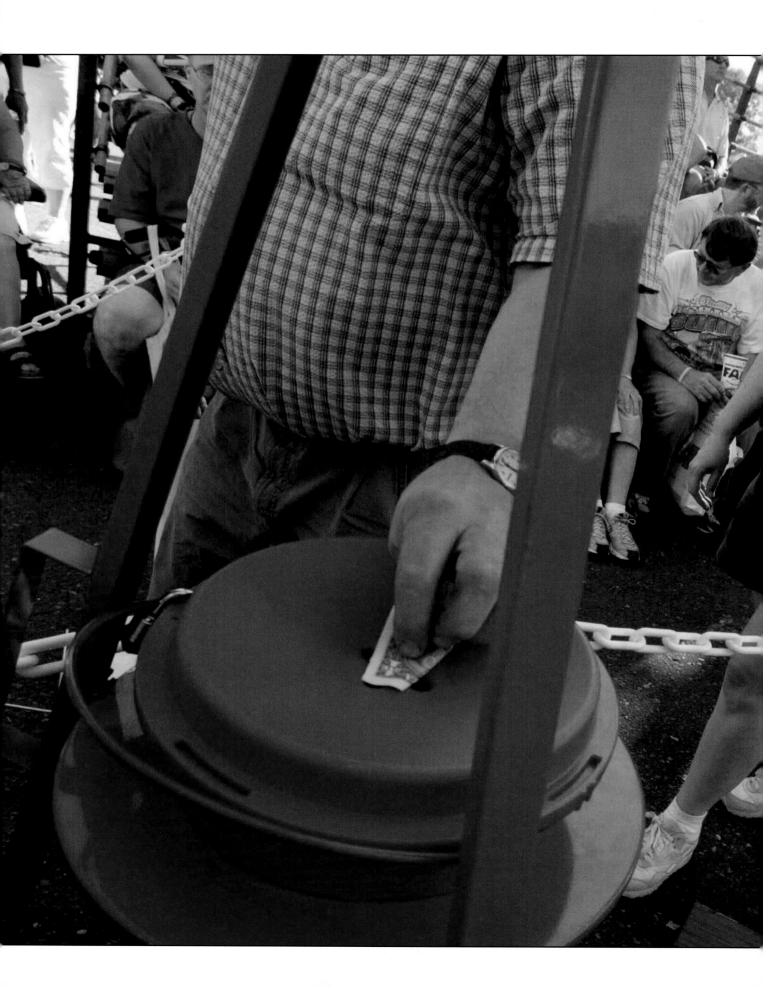

Americans race to give to charities

September 6, 2005
By Aleksandrs Rozens, Associated Press

NEW YORK—Within a week after news and images of the chaos left by Hurricane Katrina were broadcast, Americans donated over half a billion dollars to charities aiding victims of the flood.

The speed of the money raised has outpaced the rate of donations offered to victims of the 2001 terror attacks and could hit $1 billion, according Stacy Palmer, the editor of *The Chronicle of Philanthropy*, a publication that tracks nonprofit organizations.

"It is unprecedented in scale and speed," Palmer said.

"This outpaces anything we have had," said Ryland Dodge, a spokesman with the American Red Cross. "The 9-11 donations ended up being $1 billion dollars (collected) over a long period of time."

By far the largest single corporate donation has come from Wal-Mart, the retail giant, which donated $17 million late last week. In addition, the Walton Family Foundation, a foundation created by the family of the founder of Wal-Mart, donated $15 million to a variety of organizations.

Also, the retail giant has donated over $3 million in merchandise donations like clothing, water, diapers and toothbrushes that were shipped to shelters.

Above: Omaha native and Tulane University first-year medical student Nicole Gilg collects donations in Omaha, Nebraska, for the Hurricane Katrina relief fund. Gilg evacuated New Orleans before the hurricane struck.

Much of the money has been donated to the American Red Cross, which had received $409 million as of midday Tuesday. The Salvation Army had raised $50 million by Tuesday afternoon allowing it to serve as many as 500,000 meals a day at its canteens.

Each meal costs $3, according to Melissa Temme, a spokeswoman for The Salvation Army.

The pace of giving has been so hectic at the Salvation Army that online donations have, in the four days after the hurricane, surpassed what has been raised over the Internet in five years.

Other corporations offering donations included General Electric Co. which gave $6 million to the Red Cross and The Coca-Cola Co. which gave $5 million to the Red Cross as well as other charities, Palmer said.

"It is unprecedented in scale and speed."

−Stacy Palmer, editor of
The Chronicle of Philanthropy

Above: University of Illinois staff member Vera Mainz holds the donation box up for Abby Winstead of Morton, Illinois, on the shoulders of her father Cory Winstead. Students and staff members were collecting donations for Hurricane Katrina victims at each entrance before the start of the Illinois/Rutgers football game at Champaign's Memorial Stadium.

Much of the pace of giving stepped up on Thursday and Friday as images of the devastation and the plight of people in the stricken areas became evident.

"People are very frustrated when they see the slowness of the response (to the hurricane). People figure they can give a gift very quickly," said Palmer, adding that some corporations have increased the size of their donations in response to the images of devastation. "The slowness of the response is part of what triggered this outpouring of donations."

The pool of religious groups announcing plans to help has grown. Muslim groups like Kind Hearts, Islamic Relief and the Muslim American Society announced the formation of the Muslim Hurricane Relief Task Force, which will coordinate $10 million pledged by the groups for victims of Hurricane Katrina.

That aid would be distributed regardless of religious faith, said Ibrahim Hooper, spokesman at the Council of American-Islamic Relations, a Washington-based advocacy group.

Above: Bisher Kaddoura (right) of North Bergen, New Jersey, holds a box to collect donations as Muslims leave the Islamic Center of Passaic County after prayers. The donations are part of a nationwide call for U.S. Muslims to help the hurricane victims.

Above: The American Red Cross is facilitating nationwide donations to the Hurricane Katrina Disaster Relief fund. In Los Angeles, commuters stop by Dodger Stadium to give money.

Right: Money donated by fans as they arrive at the WNBA playoff game between the Indiana Fever and New York Liberty overflows its container.

"I think the Red Cross is amazing. It's a great feeling to help the people here who have lost so much. It's everyone's duty to help however they can."

–Red Cross volunteer

Loved ones search for victims of Katrina

September 7, 2005
By Deborah Hastings, Associated Press

Rachal Watson is 19 years old and nine months pregnant. Her 1-year-old daughter is missing. So is her boyfriend. She paces the floor of a Houston motel, far from her former home in New Orleans, rubbing her belly while her worries run wild.

"I just can't take it no more," she says in a high-pitched wail. "I really can't. I have no momma and no daddy. That's the only family I have."

Her posting, on the Web's National Next of Kin Registry: "I am safe in Houston hotel looking for a baby girl."

She is one of thousands upon thousands looking for the ones they love in any way they can.

In the wreckage of Katrina, not much works, especially the phones. So desperate families try to reach the missing through television or the Internet.

Most pleas on the Web begin the same: "Where are you?" The only difference is the number of question marks.

Above: Rachal Watson sits in her Houston hotel room waiting for word on the whereabouts of her 1-year-old daughter Te-Erika and her daughter's father James Green. The three were separated from each other at the New Orleans Superdome when Rachal, who is nine months pregnant, began having labor pains.

Previous: Jean Frye of Jackson, Mississippi (right), comforts her cousins Geselle Henry of Slidell, Louisiana (left), and Gwendolyn Crockett of Westnego, Louisiana, displaced by Hurricane Katrina.

Right: Holding back tears, Violet "Chubby" Guerra stands outside a Dallas bus station holding a sign listing family members who went missing during Hurricane Katrina.

Eleanor Sawyer of New Orleans writes, "I am staying at the Hirsch Coliseum in Shreveport, Louisiana and I looking for my son Darrell Sawyer ..."

On another site, Patty Hein looks for her sister and brother-in-law, from Long Beach, Miss. "Any info about where they lived, if it's intact, any word, we are so worried," she wrote.

On the Web site of the National Center for Missing and Exploited Children, photographs have been posted of 20 Louisiana children whose parents are missing.

Some are toddlers. Others are teenagers. Most are in between—8, 9, 10 years old. The youngest grin at the camera. The teenagers try hard not to look scared. The kids in the middle just look bewildered.

On national television, relatives stand in front of the Houston Astrodome and other evacuation sites, holding cardboard signs bearing names of the missing and phone numbers for them to call.

Others look directly into camera lenses and beg for information, or try to give it.

"Your mother and daddy are headed for the convention center," said Bettie Perrier of New Orleans, as she headed for a bus, trailing tears of frustration. "We don't know what we'll do there."

Trina Sutton, looking angry and frantic, stood outside the Astrodome and recited her phone number on CNN. She was separated from her two children, Marice and

Left: Kathleen LaFrance combs Houston's Astrodome, searching for her husband and 14-year-old son.

Opposite: Many of the Gulf Coast's hurricane survivors were separated from loved ones during rescue operations and are desperately seeking word of their well-being.

Deverenisha, as they were being evacuated. She has no idea where they are. "No one can't tell me nothing," she said.

After a week, Angie Holman in Jacksonville, Fla., had given up hope. Four family members in the New Orleans area, including one who is blind and diabetic, hadn't been heard from. Hamon had registered their names on every Web site she could find. She monitored television news broadcasting, searching the background for faces she recognized.

"I would just be looking to see if I could see someone who belonged to me," she said. "It's just the not knowing and not being able to do anything. We were helpless. We all just wanted to get in the car and go, or get on a plane and fly down there. But where would we go? What would we do? How would we look for them?"

"Where are you?"

–Repeated question on missing evacuees website

On Monday, just before midnight, the Red Cross called Holman's grandmother.

"They're all accounted for. They're in some kind of shelter in Lafayette, La. They're all together," Holman said Tuesday, her voice breaking in relief and exhaustion. "We haven't been able to speak with them, but they're OK. They lost everything, but they got out with their lives." And then there is Rachal Watson, who thought things couldn't get much worse than having to live in the Louisiana Superdome without power or food or water. She dove under a National Guard truck when people in the surging crowd outside shot at rescue helicopters. "I was so scared I forgot I was pregnant," she said. "I landed on my stomach, like a baseball slide."

Not long after, she started having contractions. She was taken by ambulance to New Orleans' airport. "The wouldn't let my baby or my boyfriend on the ambulance. They said I had to get on by myself."

She hasn't seen either one of them since. And she hasn't given birth.

As Tuesday wore on, she got a little bit of news about her boyfriend. There was a James Green, born in 1988, registered by the Red Cross at a San Antonio shelter. Babies weren't being registered by name, she was told.

The charity that flew her to Houston, the Paul Alan Caldwell Foundation, is sending someone to walk through the shelter, looking for James Green.

"I know it's him," she said, though Green is a common name. "I know it's him."

Left: Nineteen-month-old twins Starr and Skye Toca wait outside Reunion Arena with their parents, who hope to reunite with a cousin they heard was sheltered there.

Opposite: Jaylen Moore, 10, hugs his great-grandmother Jane Carroll after arriving in Chicago and being reunited with his family after they fled their home in Gulfport, Mississippi.

Below: Nikolle Johnson (center) is greeted by family members Stacy Nolan (left) and Cynthia Henry in Addison, Texas. Johnson arrived in Texas by private jet, with Nolan's 7-month-old son.

In Mississippi, some want out, others to rebuild

September 5, 2005
By Vicki Smith, Associated Press

BILOXI, Mississippi—The people who have chosen to stay or are stuck in demolished communities along the Mississippi coast scavenge for basics each day, as convoys of soldiers and supplies pass them by, headed for the nearly empty city of New Orleans.

Some are staying with the hope of rebuilding their communities. Others say they would leave if only they could get a ride. All agree that with no water or power, probably for months to come, they need more help from the government just to survive.

"I have been all over the world. I've been in a lot of Third World countries where people were better off than the people here are right now," retired Air Force Capt. William Bissell said Monday.

The official death toll in Mississippi stood at 160 and rising Monday. More than 17,000 people were living in American Red Cross shelters in the state, with thousands more in hotels and storm-damaged homes.

Virginia Fisher tried to stay in a shelter, but she left when people started getting sick with a stomach virus.

"I know I'm better off here," she says of her home. It's uninhabitable and reeking, but she and Buford Fisher are living in it anyway, holding fast to what little community they have left.

Each morning, people in their neighborhood gather food and water from private donors and scattered aid stations and congregate in the Fishers' yard to divvy it up.

"We got 22 people coming here for food and water," Fisher said. "As long as I'm here, they're going to come here."

Above: Work crews begin to clean up the Katrina's wreckage in Gulfport, Mississippi.
Previous: James Smith wades past a building destroyed by Hurricane Katrina in Gulfport
Opposite: Mississippi State Narcotics Bureau officer Chuck Harris erects an American flag found among the debris in Waveland, Mississippi.

"Unfortunately, I am from Mississippi mud and I will stay here. No matter how many times we leave, we always come back."

—Cyndi Mathews, Katrina survivor

Lavone Lollar, 34, and her three children have been living with 75 others in an Ocean Springs shelter that smells like dirty diapers. She would leave "in a heartbeat" if she had a way.

"The roads are so backed up and everybody's still fighting for gas," she said. Most people in the shelter don't have cars, "so we're having to wait for people to come to us instead of us going to them."

She fears the psychological toll the disaster is taking on those slowly realizing they've lost everything.

"You talk to somebody one minute, they're OK," she said. "The next, the devil's starting to get into them."

Mississippi Emergency Management Agency director Robert Latham said his agency will work with local authorities and the Red Cross to help people who want to relocate. Alabama has offered room for about 2,500 in shelters or hotels.

For those who want to stay, Mississippi officials say they will eventually offer temporary housing in tents or in 20,000 small trailers that have been ordered.

Many residents, old and new, said they would never leave the area, because they wanted to help bring it back.

"I'm only leaving if they make me. This is my home," said Glen Ridgeway, 53, who moved here from Ohio to find work five years ago. "I'm not afraid of doing the dirty jobs along with the good jobs."

Cyndi Mathews, 30, would like to leave her shelter in Ocean Springs, but she has nowhere to go.

"Unfortunately, I am from Mississippi mud and I will stay here," she said. "No matter how many times we leave, we always come back."

Left: A bulldozer begins the mammoth task of clearing Hurricane Katrina's handiwork in Long Beach, Mississippi.

Opposite: The span of Highway 90 leading into Biloxi, Mississippi, is completely impassable after being dismantled by the hurricane.

U.S. students displaced by Katrina find new schools

September 8, 2005
By AFP

ZACHARY, Louisiana (AFP)—Six-year-old Megan Treme entered her new classroom clutching her stuffed kitten Angelcake to her side as if it were her last friend.

"I'm nervous," she said.

Northwestern Elementary School here is a long way from her home in Slidell, La., just one of many communities in the southern state devastated by Hurricane Katrina.

Megan is one of the luckier of the 200,000 children in Louisiana whose schools were damaged or destroyed by what is shaping up to become the worst natural disaster in U.S. history. State officials have said it would be at least several days before most of the students displaced by the storm can resume their education.

Flooding caused by Katrina was so severe that most schools in the New Orleans metropolitan area of 1.4 million people are likely to remain closed through the entire school year, said Cecil Picard, the Louisiana state school superintendent.

Those students, referred to as "Katrina's kids," are spread out in shelters, hotels and temporary homes across the United States. Some will likely never return home.

Picard has asked schools throughout the nation to take these children as quickly as possible. Most already have been away from class since Aug. 29, when Katrina pounded Louisiana and two other states along the Gulf Coast.

Megan; her mother, Melody Treme; and an aunt are among hundreds of storm evacuees who have taken refuge in Zachary, a city of 13,000 north of the state capital of Baton Rouge.

As Treme talked with teacher Lynn Hendry, Megan eagerly pulled out a puzzle shaped like a map of the United States, dumped the pieces on the floor and began putting it together with the help of assistant principal Sandy Davis.

Treme said her daughter is eager to get back to school. "She does really well," she said.

She is one of about 200 children who have already been placed in Northwestern Elementary and the city's other three schools, city school Superintendent Warren Drake said. The school system also has hired three displaced teachers and expects to hire three more, he said.

He said leaders of the school system, which normally has about 3,500 students and is already overcrowded, decided to move quickly to aid the displaced children when classes resumed Tuesday for the first time since the storm.

"We're putting them in and worrying about the paperwork later," he said. "We have to help these people. They didn't ask to come here and we're going to do the right thing."

Camryn Key, 5, of New Orleans is one of two displaced students in Janet

> *"We're putting them in and worrying about the paperwork later. We have to help these people."*
>
> —Zachary School Superintendent Warren Drake

—

Previous: Sarah Atherton (left) and Cherie Ward of the Red Cross lead children from New Orleans to lunch at Camp Williams in Riverton, Utah. The state has asked for a federal waiver so the 42 school-age children at Camp Williams can attend classes in a one-room-schoolhouse setting while remaining near their parents at the Utah Army National Guard base.

Opposite: Graham Williams (left) puts his arm around his new schoolmate, Jameall Gatlin, at a Houston elementary school. Jameall's family evacuated New Orleans and plan to make Houston their new home.

Above: Kiana Williams (left) looks on as her aunt, Joy Stacker, registers her daughter Diamond Washington (not pictured) to attend school in Baton Rouge, Louisiana. Williams and her daughter Asia Lola Williams (second from right) along with Stacker and Washington were residents of New Orleans and lost everything in the hurricane.

Previous: Former New Orleans residents Joneisha Smith, 5, (foreground) and her sister, Tyrienisha, 10, look over their school supplies in the lobby of their hotel in Sterling Heights, Michigan.

Thorne's kindergarten class. She said she and her parents are staying with her maternal grandmother in Zachary.

"I'm going to stay here until the storm comes away from New Orleans," she said.

Thorne, knowing how long that might take, has made Camryn feel at home. She has her own special seat at one of the tables in the class and her name is among those written on hearts on a poster hanging from the ceiling.

Parents have expressed concern about funding and stability of classroom assignments, but the community understands the need for displaced children to quickly return to a normal life after the storm, Thorne said.

"We'll make room for everyone," she said.

The state government has authorized temporary schools to open in shelters and vacant buildings to ease crowding, and Drake said he was considering an offer to set up classes for younger children at a local church shelter.

"We'll make room for everyone."

–Janet Thorne, Teacher

He said he would work out funding issues later with U.S. and state officials. Both governments have promised to aid school districts that take in hurricane refugees.

World pledges aid to victims

September 3, 2005
By AFP

The world's industrialized countries agreed today to tap their strategic oil reserves and pour 60 million barrels into the market in a month to cope with disruptions in the aftermath of Hurricane Katrina.

The International Energy Agency said that all its 26 member states had agreed to take "collective action in response to the interrupted oil supplies in the Gulf of Mexico caused by Hurricane Katrina."

North Atlantic Treaty Organization chief Jaap de Hoop Scheffer said NATO also stood ready to contribute.

Among the major allies:

• Australia promised $7.5 million through the American Red Cross.

"Given the extraordinary generosity of the United States when other countries are in need, and given the very close relationship between Australia and the United States, and given also the scale of the disaster, we believe it is a very valuable gesture and a mark of our concern for the scale of the human misery that has come from this disaster," said Prime Minister John Howard.

• British Prime Minister, Tony Blair, said he had spoken to George Bush, and Britain was ready to help "in any way that we can."

"The whole of this country feels for the people of the Gulf Coast of America who have been afflicted by what is a terrible, terrible natural tragedy," he said in a speech in Watford, England.

"We want to express our sympathy and our solidarity and give our prayers and thoughts to the people who were affected by what has happened out there on the Gulf Coast," he said.

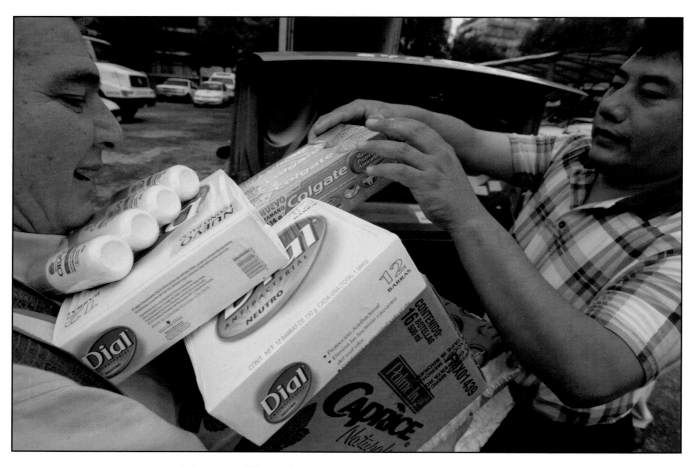

Above: A Red Cross volunteer is loaded with donations from a man at the Mexican Red Cross center in Mexico City.

- Germany's Foreign Minister, Joschka Fischer, met U.S. ambassador to Germany, William Robert Timken, and said he had made firm offers of "medicine, water treatment and technology to help find survivors" on behalf of the German government.
- The French foreign ministry offered eight aircraft and two ships, with 600 tents and 1,000 camp beds also available at the United States' request.
- Japan offered $200,000 for the American Red Cross and up to $300,000 worth of tents, blankets, power generators and water tanks. Toyota offered $5 million, Nissan $500,000.
- The Canadian Defense Minister, Bill Graham, said his country was preparing a package, including an offer of military assets. Canada will also boost oil exports to the United States.
- Among others, the Netherlands, a low-lying country that depends on its system of levees, or dams, has offered to send a team of experts to help plan the reconstruction of New Orleans. Italy said it was ready to help but had not been contacted. Sweden offered medical and technical aid. Lithuania's Red Cross started taking donations, and Denmark said it had ordered emergency management officials "to look into the possibilities of sending aid."

Switzerland offered help in reconstruction or the prevention of further catastrophes as well as high-power pumps and other equipment. The Spanish arm of the Red Cross said it was sending a team of logistical personnel.

Venezuela offered the U.S. embassy in Caracas money, fuel and medical and other aid.

"The U.S. Red Cross has asked for aid from 50 to 70 logistical personnel from the International Federation of Red Cross and Red Crescent Societies," the Spanish organization said.

"In response to this call the Spanish Red Cross has mobilized around 200 logisticians trained in emergency situations and between four and 10 could leave for the southeastern United States within hours."

More poignant were offers from the needy.

Sri Lanka—still recovering from the December 26 tsunami that devastated the island's coastlines and killed 31,000 people—said it had donated $25,000 and asked doctors to help the relief effort.

Somalis offered sympathy.

"New Orleans looks like Mogadishu when the war started," said bus driver Aden Mohamud in Somalia's war-shattered capital.

He said he was troubled by television images that showed most of the some 300,000 desperate people still trapped in New Orleans were black.

"Maybe some whites are also starving, but the African Americans are who I have seen," Mohamud said. "I am sorry they are poor like us."

"The whole of this country feels for the people of the Gulf Coast of America who have been afflicted by what is a terrible, terrible natural tragedy,"

–British Prime Minister Tony Blair

Evacuees across the country

September 10, 2005
By AFP

As of September 12, 2005, an estimated 377,700 Hurricane Katrina refugees was in shelters, hotels, homes and other housing in 33 states and Washington D.C., according to the Red Cross and state officials:

TEXAS: An estimated 205,000 in shelters and homes

LOUISIANA: About 54,000 in 240 shelters, 659 in special needs shelters

ARKANSAS: About 50,000 in shelters, motels and homes

TENNESSEE: 15,500

MISSISSIPPI: 13,262 in 104 Red Cross shelters

MISSOURI: Nearly 6,100 in homes, hotels and church camps

FLORIDA: 3,472 in 48 shelters

ALABAMA: 2,183 in shelters; 660 in hotels; 116 in state parks; more in homes

KENTUCKY: 116 at Murray camp in western Kentucky, plus estimated 3,100 statewide

OKLAHOMA: 2,352 in four shelters

INDIANA: At least 70 in two shelters; more than 2,000 statewide

ILLINOIS: More than 2,000

MARYLAND: About 2,000 seeking Red Cross or local assistance

VIRGINIA: 1,841

NORTH CAROLINA: 450 in shelters, at least 1,381 in other housing

Above: A nun plays foosball, at St. Catherine's Convent in Houston, with boys evacuated from New Orleans. The nuns converted their convent into a shelter for survivors of Hurricane Katrina.

Previous: A sign decorates the sleeping quarters of Dominick Geraci (right) of New Orleans and provides a little levity at the Hurricane Katrina refugee shelter in Hattiesburg, Mississippi.

GEORGIA: 1,384 staying in 11 Red Cross shelters

OHIO: About 20 in two Red Cross shelters, at least 1,357 staying in hotels and with family and friends

MINNESOTA: 1,000, plus 54 families with Red Cross chapters

COLORADO: About 350 in one Red Cross shelter, plus more than 700

SOUTH CAROLINA: 239 in one shelter, 800 in hotels, 228 in Charleston hotels

CALIFORNIA: 807 families in hotels and one Red Cross shelter

KANSAS: About 800, mostly in hotels and homes

MICHIGAN: 216 at Fort Custer Training Center, Red Cross assisting 300 families

NEW MEXICO: 28 at the Albuquerque Convention Center, more than 450 statewide

NEW JERSEY: About 400 staying with relatives or in motels.

UTAH: About 300 people at Utah Army National Guard's Camp Williams

ARIZONA: 347 in two shelters

WEST VIRGINIA: 308 at National Guard Camp Dawson

NEW YORK: 303 cases in Red Cross shelters

MASSACHUSETTS: 209 at Camp Edwards, plus more than 40 families

PENNSYLVANIA: At least 200 in homes, shelters and other locations

DISTRICT OF COLUMBIA: About 200 people at a Red Cross shelter

WISCONSIN: 200 people in one shelter

RHODE ISLAND: 106 in Navy housing, 75 in hotels and homes

Right: A weary 5-year-old, Christallie Ewing, waits with her grandmother at the Salvation Army shelter in Biloxi, Mississippi.

Dear America,

I suppose we should introduce our-selves: We're South Louisiana. . . . First of all, we thank you. For your money, your water, your food, your prayers, your boats and buses and the men and women of your National Guards, fire departments, hospitals and everyone else who has come to our rescue. We're a fiercely proud and independent people, and we don't cotton much to outside interference, but we're not ashamed to accept help when we need it. And right now, we need it. . . . When all this is over and we move back home, we will repay to you the hospitality and generosity of spirit you offer to us in this season of our despair.

That is our promise. That is our faith.

—Chris Rose, The *Times-Picayune*
excerpted from "Dear America"

Right: The playing field of Houston's Astrodome is covered with cots and evacuees from hurricane-ravaged New Orleans.

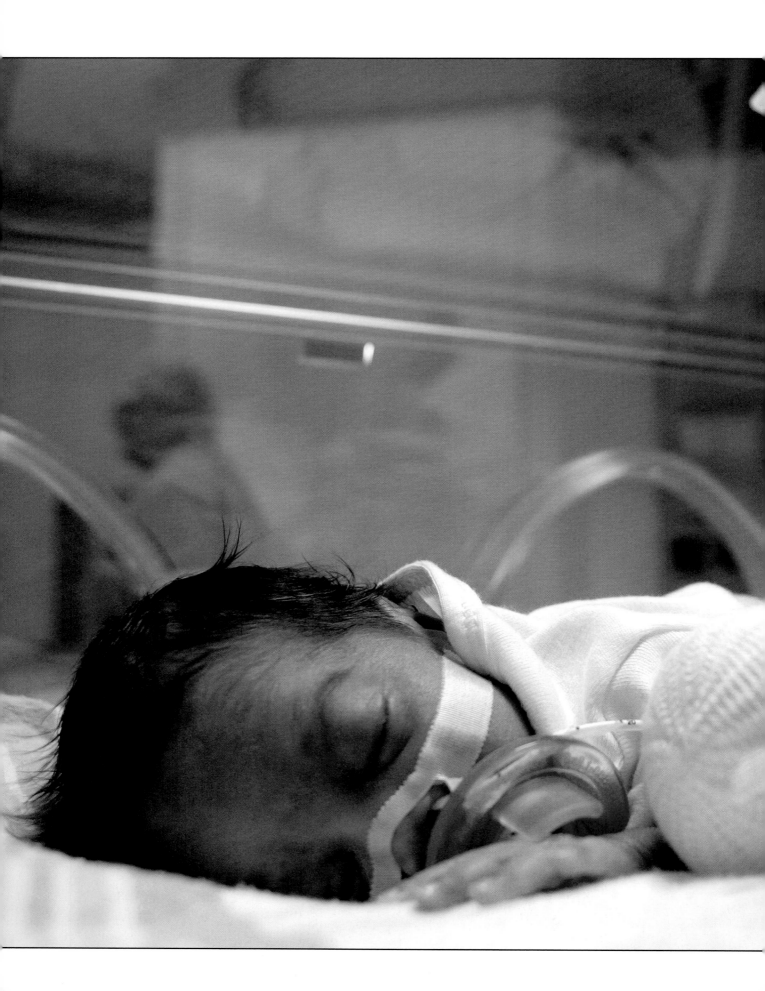

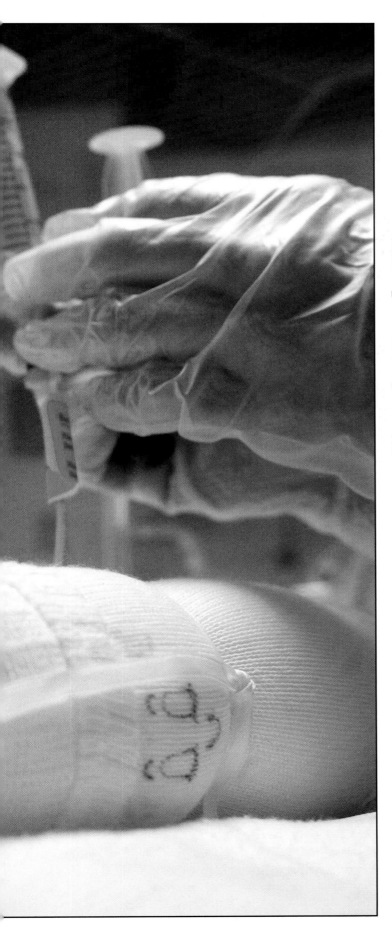

Reuniting the youngest survivors with their families

September 12, 2005
By Susan Moyer

Orphans of the storm. A safe shelter set up for missing children is 80 miles from New Orleans, but for the children who have been separated from their parents, it is a frightening place. They don't know where their parents are. Volunteers are trying to reunite all of the children with their parents, and success stories are surfacing daily.

Pictures of the missing youngsters stare out from the Web site of the National Center for Missing and Exploited Children, but a spokesman for the center said that they were the tip of an iceberg.

But in red capital letters stamped across the portraits of seven children on a missing children's Web site, the word RESOLVED ends a story that moved many adults to tears in despair but eventually with relief.

Six-year-old Diamonte Love, carrying a baby, bravely led five other children to safety. He was wandering down a raised highway in New Orleans being trailed through crowds on Causeway Boulevard by five exhausted toddlers.

The little group was taken by ambulance to a shelter in Baton Rouge where they were fed, rested, and coaxed into talking. Social workers doubted they had been abandoned because it appeared that they had been well cared for. Diamonte was able to provide the names of all of the children, but at first when he said his mother's name was Katrina, the volunteers didn't believe that could be true. Two long days passed without word from the children's parents.

Then Diamonte's mother, Catrina Williams, saw her children's pictures on the Internet. She had handed them to a rescue helicopter hovering over her home several days before, she said, having been told that the helicopter would return for adults. It never did. Ms. Williams, 26, was evacuated to San Antonio, to where an executive jet laid on by a charity flew all seven children on Sunday.

Another encouraging reunion story is of Barren Snell, a premature baby born two months early who was still hospitalized when Hurricane Katrina struck New Orleans. Along with 120 other infants in the city's hospitals, he was evacuated to the neonatal intensive care unit at Woman's Hospital in Baton Rouge. The electricity was out, and the hurricane made travel perilous for the young survivors. Along the way, Barren was separated from his mother.

The babies began arriving at the Baton Rouge hospital as floodwaters rose in New Orleans. They came by ambulance, car and helicopter. Armed guards sometimes accompanied the convoys because of shootings in the city.

Reuniting the babies with their families has kept social workers very busy. The names and phone numbers for the parents were in the babies' medical records, but the numbers were in New Orleans, where there is no longer phone service.

The babies lay in their tiny beds waiting to be reunited with their families. Pink paper cutouts in the shape of the hurricane above their beds read: "We weathered the storm, Hurricane Katrina, 2005."

One by one, the 121 infants were reunited with their parents. All except Barren.

Happily, Barren's mother and siblings were found after being marooned in an apartment surrounded by floodwaters without food or drinking water. They stayed alive on a little food and water that a neighbor had shared with them.

Previous: Tiny survivor Alysa Blackwell is one of over 200 babies evacuated from hospitals in New Orleans and brought to the intensive care units of Woman's Hospital in Baton Rouge, Louisiana.
Opposite: New Orleans evacuee Bunne Burke feeds her newborn son, Skylar, at Woman's Hospital.

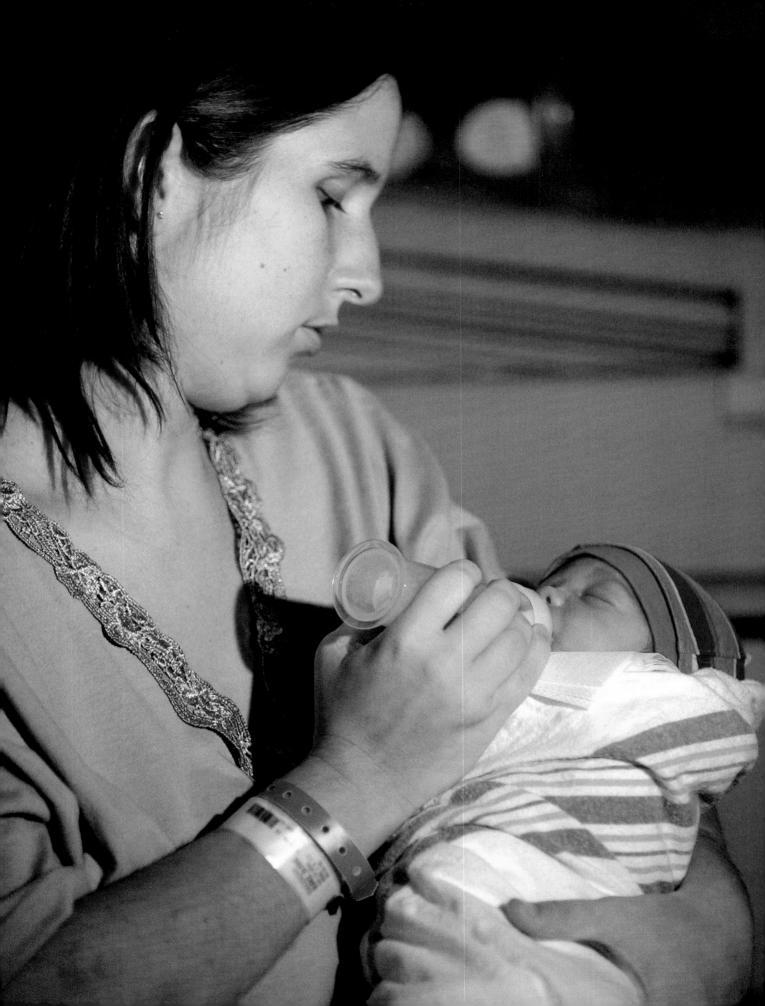

Above: Vondrice Jacque, of New Orleans, and his son, Vonjaveah, take a nap together at a shelter in Hattiesburg, Mississippi.

Right: Nurse Melanie Perkins comforts preemie Alysa Blackwell at Woman's Hospital.

Opposite: Celebrating the miraculous evacuation of over 200 babies, this sign adorns the incubator of one of the tiniest hurricane survivors.

Quilters for Katrina is dedicated to the smallest victims of Katrina. We are individuals who wish to make a contribution of love in addition to any other kind of aid we can offer. Our goal is to provide infants and toddlers with their own handmade comfort blanket. This is a great opportunity for anyone who is chairbound and who wishes to make a difference. Anyone with a sewing machine can put it to use now by helping us to make desperately needed baby blankets. If you have ever made a "Quillo," e-mail Julia Fleming at juliaflem@cox.net.

Barren's mother hung signs out of the windows of the apartment and waved towels trying to attract the attention of helicopters overhead. A soldier eventually heard their cries for help and they were rescued and evacuated to the New Orleans airport.

Ecstatic that her 3-month-old is alive and unharmed, Snell is unsure of what the future holds for her little family, or where they will go next.

Officials at shelters say they've received hundreds of calls from frantic parents. And they are giving firm hope and reassurances that they will continue to work to bring all of the families back together again.

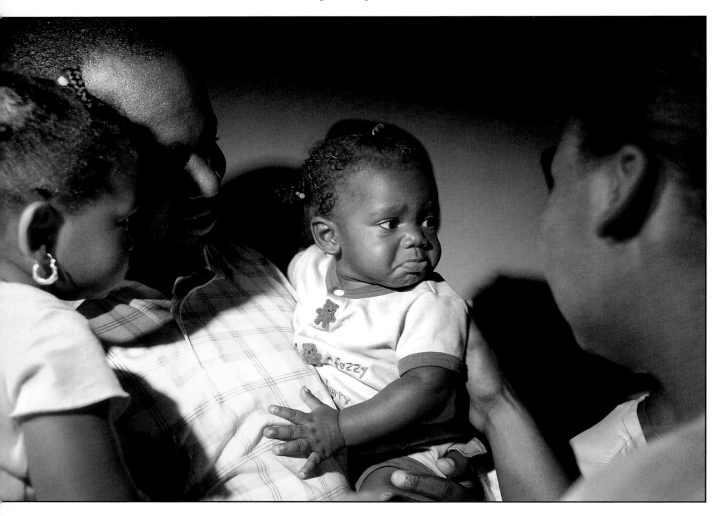

Above: Seven-month-old A'Mahd Magee is reunited with his family after arriving in Texas by private plane.

Above: The Felder family from New Orleans makes their way through Sky Harbor International Airport in Phoenix after being reunited. The parents, Christine and Johnny, were evacuated to Phoenix and became separated from their four children, who were evacuated to Houston.

"My family is still together—we are alive. The Red Cross welcomed us with open arms. We don't know what is next ... but we are together. It is good to be safe!"

–Katrina survivor

People helping animals, animals helping people

September 8, 2005
By Susan Moyer

The human survivors of Hurricane Katrina have suffered unimaginably. The pictures and video from the entire Gulf Coast are heartbreaking, and finding relief for them comes first. But right after them come all of the animals that were left behind. Many of Katrina's victims will be those least able to help themselves—animals.

So who will be there for the pets lost and injured after this devastating storm? Organizations across the country have mobilized to provide aid and facilitate reunions between pets and their owners.

Veterinary Medical Assistance Teams (VMAT), established by the American Veterinary Medical Association (AVMA) and funded primarily by the American Veterinary Medical Foundation (AVMF), are working as part of the Federal Emergency Management Agency (FEMA) National Disaster Medical System (NDMS) to care for injured animals.

VMAT personnel consist of veterinarians, veterinary technicians, scientists, epidemiologists, toxicologists, pathologists, pharmacists and other support technicians trained to assist the local veterinary communities and provide medical care to injured animals, coordinate animal relief efforts on site and address public health issues.

There is a lot of work to do. First rescuers need to rescue and tend to the animals, and then there is the huge task of reuniting them with their families.

There is a busy chat room at nola.com, the Web site attached to the Times-Picayune newspaper. As soon as the chat room opened, there were thousands of messages from people who care about animals. Many of them are looking for their pets.

Animal rescue operations in the hardest hit areas of Mississippi and Louisiana increased dramatically as rescue workers gained access to more of the devastated areas. As rescue efforts increase, there are more success stories of animals being reunited with their owners. Pet owners were encouraged to call the animal rescue hotlines to provide descriptions of lost pets and, if owners looking for lost pets are still in the area, to stop by the shelter to look for their animals.

The outpouring of support from the animal welfare community, corporations and the public has been phenomenal. The ASPCA has been inundated with inquiries from the public about what they can do to help. One man pledged the use of a cargo plane to fly animals out of the disaster area when needed and the use of his farm in Nebraska to house animals.

The Best Friends Animal Society and its sister sanctuary St. Francis Animal Sanctuary set up emergency housing for animals rescued from metro New Orleans. Capital Animal Care, a Washington D.C.-based nonprofit animal welfare organization donated its state-of-the-art vet mobile clinic to Best Friends Animal Society's animal rescue operation base in Tylertown, Mississippi.

The American Humane Association is working with several animal welfare organizations to find, rescue and care for the hundreds of animals still stranded or unaccounted for after the hurricane. Many American Humane volunteers are caring for pets at a temporary animal shelter in Lafayette, La. Other American Humane volunteers are in New Orleans with boats, gear and specialized skills to rescue animals in flooded areas.

The Louisiana Department of Agriculture and Forestry, the Louisiana Society for the Prevention of Cruelty to Animals (LA/SPCA), the Louisiana Veterinary Medical Association (LVMA), the Louisiana Animal Control Association (LACA) and the LSU School of Veterinary Medicine (SVM) managed animal evacuations and recovery plans

Previous: Lisa Hochstetler with United Canine, a volunteer search group from Ohio, and her dog Grizzly search for victims of Hurricane Katrina in East Biloxi, Mississippi.

Opposite: Kewah Yee gives a stray puppy some water from an artesian spring tap in Slidell, Louisiana.

Above: Carroll Zehner kisses her pet guinea pig, left in their home during the hurricane, after returning to Jefferson Parish for the first time since the storm.

for New Orleans pets and displaced animals, including managing a hotline for identifying pets needing rescue, coordinating the activities of professional animal rescue volunteers and assisting with emergency animal shelter operations throughout the state.

The Humane Society of the United States is the leading national humane group working in Mississippi under the direction of the Board of Animal Health. Their support teams have set up major staging areas in the coastal county of Jackson near Gautier and in Hattiesburg to serve as their primary operational bases.

Some canine evacuees evacuated from the Gulf Coast have a new home at the Washington Animal Rescue League. The first arrivals included 22 dogs that endured an 18-hour van ride from Louisiana. Previously they had spent several days in an overflow animal shelter. Area residents who heard about the arrival of the furry evacuees stopped by with donations of toys and food for the dogs.

Veterinarians from the Washington Animal Rescue League have been in the gulf region performing surgery on rescued animals and providing other medical care.

The outpouring of care and support for the four-legged survivors has been overwhelming, swamping phone lines and knocking out Web sites with the heavy demand.

And animals, in return, are aiding the survivors of Hurricane Katrina. Although the devastating effects of Katrina continue to mount and the estimated death toll climbs, the heroic canine disaster search teams, trained by the National Disaster Search Dog Foundation, are once again being called to national duty. National Disaster Search Dog

Above: Recon gets a drink of water from Jim Boggeri of the Oakland California Task Force 4 search and rescue team while searching for victims of Hurricane Katrina in East Biloxi, Mississippi.

Foundation is a nonprofit organization whose mission to produce the most highly trained canine disaster search teams in the nation.

Not since 9/11 have so many urban search and rescue canines be activated to one disaster to do what they do best—find the survivors—who may be trapped in the houses, mobile homes and other structures destroyed by Katrina.

The task forces are composed of a team of first responders trained to perform rescue operations after major disasters. A key component of that team is the search and rescue dog. Typically, the dogs will clear an area to make sure no one has been left alive in the debris. The dogs' remarkable senses of smell and abilities to safely navigate dangerous terrain make search dogs an invaluable asset to the search and rescue efforts.

In Tampa, Fla., Canine Unit Squad member Roger Picard and dog Jessie were among 63 Bay Area rescuers who headed for the Gulf Coast the day before Hurricane Katrina hit. They knew they could help. Jesse is a yellow labrador retriever, and she may be the Bay Area's best trained search dog. She and Picard were sent to Ground Zero in New York City after September 11. They've aided search teams in the aftermath of three hurricanes in Florida last year and following Hurricane Dennis this summer. Picard said he'd never seen anything like the devastation from Katrina.

Therapy dogs are also assisting the survivors of Hurricane Katrina by providing emotional support and friendly faces to those in shelters. The primary objective of the therapy dog and handler is to provide comfort and companionship by sharing the dog with the patients in hospitals, nursing homes and other institutions and wherever else the therapy

Vancouver Urban Search and Rescue Team members Barley (right) and Cooper wait with their handler Flynn Lamont at the Vancouver International Airport. The exhausted 46-member crew, which had gone 30 hours without sleep, was New Orleans' first wave of relief.

dog is needed. This is done in a way that increases emotional well being, promotes healing and improves the quality of life for the people being visited and the staff who cares for these people.

Therapy Dogs International has at least 34 associate members located in areas directly affected by Hurricane Katrina. Media reports show that most people in those areas have lost everything and continue to endure very difficult conditions. The organization is attempting to contact members in those areas, but communication is difficult and they are welcoming donations to help provide more therapy dogs to aid survivors.

Donations are welcome and will go to TDI members directly affected by this disaster or will be used to transport TDI dogs to temporary foster homes, if necessary. They have set up a special committee of volunteer members to administer the Katrina funds and take charge of possible fostering and transferring of therapy dogs.

The best way to assist in the disaster relief efforts for pets is to make a donation to the organizations involved so that they can purchase much needed supplies and equipment for the rescue and relief efforts, and provide assistance to animal welfare groups impacted by Hurricane Katrina.

Above: Randy Fortier and Brandy McCoy give C.C. a lift back to their fishing camp in Slidell, Louisiana.

Right: Rick Lee and Ana, from Sacramento FEMA's Search and Rescue Task Force 7, search homes destroyed by Hurricane Katrina in East Biloxi.

To donate:

THERAPY DOGS
INTERNATIONAL,
INC.
88 Bartley Road
Flanders, NJ 07836
tdi@gti.net

PETFINDER
Petfinder.com Foundation
P.O. Box 16385
Tucson, AZ 85732-6385
www.petfinder.org

HUMANE SOCIETY OF
THE UNITED STATES
HSUS Disaster Relief
Fund
Dept. DRFHBM,
2100 L Street, NW,
Washington, DC 20037
www.hsus.org

AMERICAN KENNEL
CLUB COMPANION
ANIMAL RECOVERY
CORPORATION
5580 Centerview Drive
Suite 250
Raleigh , NC 27603
www.akccar.org

AMERICAN SOCIETY
FOR THE PREVEN-
TION OF CRUELTY TO
ANIMALS (ASPCA)
424 E 92nd St
New York, NY 10128
www.aspca.org

BEST FRIENDS
ANIMAL SOCIETY
5001 Angel Canyon Rd
Kanab, UT 84741
www.bestfriends.org

LOUISIANA SPCA
1319 Japonica St
New Orleans, LA 70117
www.la-spca.org

NOAH'S WISH
PO Box 997
Placerville, CA 95667

UNITED ANIMAL
NATIONS
1722 J St
Ste 321
Sacramento, CA 95814
www.uan.org

NORTH SHORE
ANIMAL LEAGE
AMERICA
Attn: Hurricane Katrina
Animal Rescue Fund
16 Lewyt St
Port Washington, NY
11050
516-883-7900 ext 833

AKC CAR Canine
Support and Relief Fund
American Kennel Club
5580 Centerview Drive
Raleigh, North Carolina
27606
800-252-7894 to make a
donation to the AKC CAR
Canine Support and Relief
Fund

Above: Veterinarian Eugene Knispel feeds his neighbor's cat in an abandoned area of New Orleans.

Right: At a shelter in Pine Bluff, Arkansas, Joshua Thornton (left) and Antoinette Tensegno pet Casey, a 7-year-old therapy dog used to help raise the spirits of hurricane survivors.

Military gets creative for evacuations

September 7, 2005
By Lolita C. Baldor, Associated Press

WASHINGTON—Deep in St. Bernard Parish, just south of New Orleans, a man stubbornly refused to leave his home, insisting he must stay with the only things he had left in the world—his two bulldogs and eight young puppies. And three friends wouldn't go anywhere without him.

So a Navy crew built a kennel at the nearby base and, with the dogs safely secured, finally persuaded the group to leave their homes. By Wednesday they were headed to a shelter in Texas—dogs and all, Navy Cmdr. Mark Scovill, the captain of the USS *Tortuga,* said Wednesday.

Unable to enforce the mandatory evacuations being ordered by local governments, the military is getting creative to persuade stubborn residents to leave their sodden, toxic neighborhoods. And for sailors on one Navy ship, that has meant everything from erecting pet shelters and dispensing medicine to biblical pleas and old-fashioned cajoling.

Above: Brad Fals leads a crate full of puppies and his dog, Harley, out of a warehouse where he had been staying with his grandfather and two other dogs in Chalmette, Louisiana. Fals refused to evacuate until they could find shelter for his pets.

Previous: U.S. Army flight surgeon Capt. Devry C. Anderson holds a pup named Chip after the dog was rescued with its owner from their flooded New Orleans home.

"Everybody's got a reason to stay," Scovill said. "You just have to appeal to whatever logic is keeping them here."

It's a delicate balance because the military troops won't force people to leave their homes.

"If the authorities in the state of Louisiana chose to use their National Guard in a state status that would certainly be permissible and their call," said Gen. Joseph Inge, the deputy commander of the Northern Command. "When this turns into a law enforcement issue, which we perceive forced evacuation is, regular troops will not be used."

So, one winning argument, said Scovill, revolves around people's pets, since many rescuers won't allow residents to take their beloved animals with them.

"The guy didn't have much to begin with and his dogs were more important than anything he had," said Scovill, in a telephone call from his ship. "He would rather stay there and be uncomfortable and miserable with his dogs than be comfortable without them."

As of Wednesday, sailors from the *Tortuga* had brought in about 50 pets, including dogs, cats and a few parrots, and put them in the newly built kennel at Naval Station

> *"Everybody's got a reason to stay. You just have to appeal to whatever logic is keeping them here."*
>
> –Navy Cmdr. Mark Scovill

Above: Cmdr. Mark H. Scovill tries to convince a man to leave his home in devastated New Orleans and take refuge aboard the USS *Tortuga*.

New Orleans. After the pet owners were given food, water, medical attention and some rest, they were reunited with their animals and usually put on buses to shelters that would accepts the pets or to meet up with other family members.

Other people were convinced to leave, Scovill said, after he told them they could use phones and e-mail on the ship to locate families or friends so they wouldn't have to go to distant shelters.

Traveling into the parish in inflatable Zodiac crafts and at times on foot, Navy teams also found more than 15 elderly people at a five-story apartment building who were refusing to leave. They had food and water, and had only heard stories about cramped and uncomfortable conditions at shelters.

Navy officers finally convinced the group to go aboard the *Tortuga,* after describing the health and infection threats around their homes, and the better shipboard conditions. Several evacuees, Scovill said, had cuts that had gotten badly infected from the polluted water.

Doctors on the ship treated the seniors and filled prescriptions for them.

The Navy has about 10,000 troops responding to the Gulf Coast disaster out of a total active-duty force there of more than 20,000. About 45,000 National Guard troops are there also.

Above: A U.S. Navy sailor helps a hurricane survivor with paperwork after she sought refuge on the USS *Tortuga.*

Opposite: A pregnant woman is airlifted from her apartment in New Orleans by Petty Officer 2nd Class Scott D. Rady of the U.S. Coast Guard.

U.S. Red Cross helps reunite hurricane victims with relatives

September 3, 2005
By AFP

WASHINGTON—The American Red Cross set up a Web site and telephone hotline to help Hurricane Katrina survivors find their relatives and let them know they are alive.

The survivors can register their names at www.familylinks.icrc.org/katrina/locate or call the free number 1-877-LOVED-1S.

Concerned relatives can also register the names of people they are looking for.

Tens of thousands of people have been evacuated to hundreds of refugee centers across the southern United States.

The effort was supported by the worldwide Red Cross and Red Crescent Movement, the American Red Cross said.

"In order to expedite this process, we have tapped into the capacity of the International Committee of Red Cross (ICRC), whose experience in connecting families separated by disaster or armed conflict is unsurpassed," the American Red Cross said.

Above: A Red Cross volunteer carries a sleeping baby in front of the Kearny High School gymnasium in San Diego, California, where 80 evacuees are being temporarily housed.

Previous: American Red Cross volunteer Maurrie Sussman (right) comforts a New Orleans evacuee in the dining area of the Veterans Memorial Coliseum in Phoenix.

Opposite: Twenty-five members of a Red Cross relief team board a Canadian Forces aircraft in Trenton, Ontario, bound for the Gulf Coast.

American Red Cross Response to Hurricane Katrina

The American Red Cross is responding to an unprecedented natural catastrophe and devoting every resource to this humanitarian relief effort. The American people can be confident the Red Cross will spare no effort to meet the needs of hundreds of thousands of Hurricane Katrina survivors.

This disaster relief operation is constantly changing. All numbers are approximate as of Sept. 13, 2005.

Since Hurricane Katrina made landfall, the Red Cross has housed more than 207,000 survivors providing nearly 1.94 million overnight stays in 709 shelters across 24 states and the District of Columbia.

- On Sunday, Sept. 11, the Red Cross housed nearly 75,000 survivors in 445 shelters across 19 states and the District of Columbia.
- Nearly 74,000 Red Cross workers from all 50 states, Puerto Rico and the Virgin Islands have responded to Katrina. During this effort, the Red Cross has trained an additional 63,000 people in specialized disaster relief skills.
- The Red Cross, in coordination with the Southern Baptist Convention, has served more than 7.6 million hot meals and more than 6.6 million snacks to survivors of Hurricane Katrina.
- The Red Cross is expanding its efforts to provide financial assistance to upward of three-quarters of a million survivors dispersed across the nation. Assistance is provided in a variety of ways, including client assistance cards, vouchers, checks and cash.
- Survivors can register for emergency financial assistance, 24 hours a day, by calling toll-free 1-800-975-7585. Due to the large number of survivors, phone lines may be overwhelmed in the first few days.
- Persons looking for loved ones can call 1-877-LOVED-1S (1-877-568-3317), or go to www.redcross.org and click on "Family Links Registry" to:
  —Register yourself
  —Register a loved one, or
  —View the existing list of registrants

More than 182,600 have been registered online and more than 110,000 have called the hotline.

- Visit www.redcross.org or www.cdc.gov for information about health strategies and preventive measures for those in affected areas.
- To date, more than 91,000 people have received Red Cross Disaster Mental Health services.

To Volunteer
- Contact your local Red Cross chapter to become a volunteer. Well-meaning individuals are urged not to report directly to the affected areas.

"Never in my life have I met people who have such divine compassion."

–Katrina survivor giving thanks to the Red Cross volunteers

To Donate
- Making a financial contribution is the best way to help, to donate:
  —Call 1-800-HELP-NOW or 1-800-257-7575 (Spanish)

Make at secure online donation at www.redcross.org
  —Visit an Official Red Cross (Cash) Donation Site (retailer locations or online)
  —Contact your local Red Cross chapter
- As of Sept. 11, 2005, it has received $584 million in gifts and pledges for the hurricane relief effort, of which an estimate $308.1 million has been received online.

The Red Cross has a four-star rating from Charity Navigator for its effective use of donations. At least 91 cents of every dollar donated to the American Red Cross goes directly to assist disaster victims.

"When you put the Red Cross vest on, the job comes to you. This is the most multitasking I've done in a long time—there's so much to do. . . . "

−Red Cross volunteer

Above: Red Cross volunteers welcome a Hurricane Katrina survivor as she arrives at the Rhode Island National Guard air base at Quonset Point with over 100 other evacuees.

Picking up the pieces, new hope in New Orleans

September 12, 2005
By AFP

NEW ORLEANS—Workers here were picking up trash yesterday, a small miracle under the circumstances. The airport opened to cargo traffic. A bullhorn-wielding volunteer led relief workers in a chorus of "Amazing Grace."

Nearly two weeks after Hurricane Katrina's onslaught, the day was marked by signs that hopelessness was beginning to lift in this shattered city. While the final toll from the disaster remains unknown, there were indications New Orleans had begun to turn a corner.

"You see the cleaning of the streets. You see the people coming out," said the volunteer with the bullhorn, Norman Flowers. "The people aren't as afraid anymore."

Flowers, deployed by the Southern Baptist Convention, stood in the bed of a pickup truck on Canal Street, leading police, firefighters and relief workers in song, punctuated by the exuberant honk of a fire truck nearby.

"This is a sign of progress," said New Orleans resident Linda Taylor, gesturing at the impromptu gathering. "Last Sunday, I couldn't find any church services. This Sunday, people have gathered together to worship."

Above: This rooftop message says it all—New Orleans will rise from the wreckage left by Katrina.
Previous: Emergency Response Team volunteers clean up debris from a flattened home in the Gulf Coast.
Opposite: A convoy of utility trucks is headed south to help restore power to areas affected by the storm.

Numerous residents were able to visit their homes for the first time, however briefly, as floodwaters receded and work crews cleared trees, debris and downed telephone poles from major streets.

Albert Gaude III, a Louisiana State University fisheries agent, was among those returning for the first time since the storm.

"They wouldn't let us in before, but we made it now and we could drive all the way here with no problem," he said.

The Louis Armstrong New Orleans International Airport reopened for cargo traffic yesterday, and limited passenger service was expected to resume Tuesday, Airport Director Roy Williams said.

Williams said he expects about 30 departures and arrivals of passenger planes a day—far below the usual 174—at the airport, where a week ago terminals became triage units and more than two dozen people died.

Trash collection began over the weekend, a service unimaginable in the apocalyptic first days after Katrina's fury battered the Gulf Coast and broke holes in two levees, flooding most of New Orleans.

Mayor Ray Nagin was asked on NBC's *Meet the Press* whether New Orleans could stage Mardi Gras in February 2006. "I haven't even thought that far out yet," he said.

But he added, "It's not out of the realm of possibilities. ... It would be a huge boost if we could make it happen."

Nagin declined to say when the city might be drained of floodwaters.

"But I always knew that once we got the pumps up, some of our significant pumps going, that we could accelerate the draining process," he said. "The big one is pumping station six, which is our most powerful pump, and I am understanding that's just about ready to go."

The city's main wastewater treatment facility will be running by today, said Sgt. John Zeller, an engineer with the California National Guard.

"We're making progress," Zeller said. "This building was underwater yesterday."

David Smith, a volunteer firefighter from Baton Rouge, said it's a sign of progress that people like him are now in New Orleans aiding the city's recovery.

"We are helping people get the medicine they need," Smith said. "People who haven't been able to get prescriptions filled. That's a big step forward."

> *"I haven't even thought that far out yet. It's not out of the realm of possibilities. ... It would be a huge boost if we could make it happen."*
>
> —New Orleans Mayor Ray Nagin on celebrating Mardi Gras 2006

Opposite: Donald Schwartz finds a tattered American flag in the debris of a house and raises it on a utility pole.

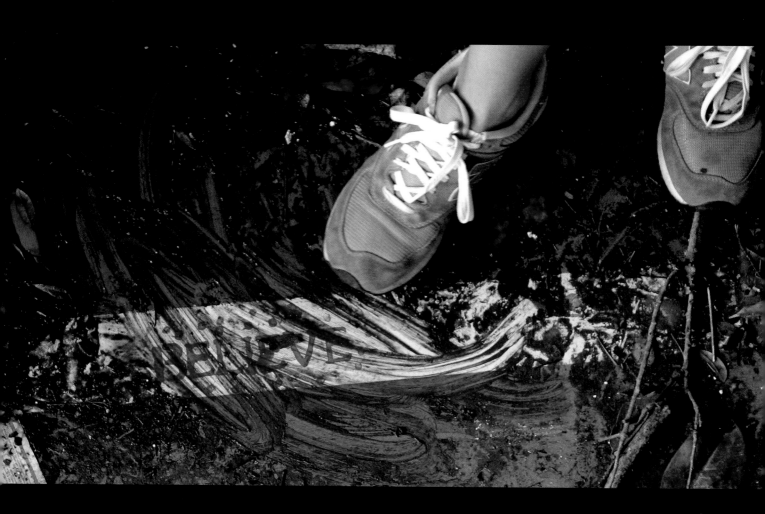

"We still don't know how many of our fellow Americans lost their lives in the Katrina catastrophe. As New Orleans Mayor Ray Nagin says, 'It is a number we all fear.' But we do know that a million did survive. They are not refugees. And I hope that everybody in this country and the world stops calling them refugees, because they are not. They are survivors, and we, the people, will not let them stand alone. They are Americans."

—Oprah Winfrey